ESSENTIAL
IT CONCEPTS
FOR SMALL
BUSINESS

ESSENTIAL IT CONCEPTS FOR SMALL BUSINESS

A Common Language Information Technology Management
Guide for Non-Technical Business Owners and Managers

Scott Brown

Ryan Creek Technology Associates, Inc.
12060 County Line Road, Suite J163
Madison, AL 35756

Published by RCTA Books.

ISBN-13: 978-0692588932
ISBN-10: 0692588930

Dedication:
To Sharon, Andrew, & Adam.

Table of Contents

Forward

The goal of this book is to provide an informative look at the dependence of small businesses on computer technology, and to help you, the small business owner or manager, understand what you need to be doing regarding your IT infrastructure and how to get it done, without first having to become a technology expert yourself.

As a much younger man, I had a hard time understanding why everyone wasn't as wowed with computers and technology as I was. Why wasn't everyone willing, even driven, to spend hours upon hours reading, learning, and experimenting with it? I was consumed and fascinated by it, and still am. For many years, they were both my vocation and avocation, and to a degree, that imbalance still exists.

However, as I have gotten older, and gained more business and life experience, I understand that not everyone is as fascinated with technology as I am. I see it exemplified when explaining to my wife about things like the latest heuristic anti-virus technology on her laptop. I no longer wonder why she doesn't look at me with awe and wonder, and demand to know more. She just wants the viruses to stay out, and she doesn't care how that is done. She wants the utility, not the burden of learning how it does what it does.

Many, if not most, small business owners and managers fall into this category, probably like yourself. They need the technology to advance their business and to compete in the marketplace with larger, more tech-savvy, competitors. What they don't need is to have to spend every waking moment trying to learn and implement the necessary technology to do so.

What I hope to do in this book is to pass on a basic understanding of the essential technologies, concepts, buzzwords, and acronyms that you, as a small business, will need to understand so that you can position yourself well in the marketplace, while remaining secure and technologically efficient. I hope to do this using plain, non-technical, language to the largest degree possible.

I hope you find something of value in this book, and take away from it the ability to analyze your business IT posture and take the necessary steps to manage it appropriately.

Scott Brown
November 25, 2015

1 Is This You?

"The number one benefit of information technology is that it empowers people to do what they want to do. It lets people be creative. It lets people be productive. It lets people learn things they didn't think they could learn before, and so in a sense it is all about potential." - Steve Ballmer

Are you a small business owner or manager that finds computers essential, but also finds them to be a burden due to their complexity? If so, read on. This book may just be the secret decoder ring you are looking for to help you know who to talk to, and what to ask them to get the most out of your technology.

Most small businesses, and their employees, are not technical in nature. At the same time, the business and the employees are almost entirely dependent on technology to do the work. Can you imagine being a salesperson without a phone, or a publisher without a word processor? Likely not. Technology is continually being introduced and you, as a small business owner or manager, need to figure out how it can help you. Therefore, a fundamental understanding of IT is essential in making basic business decisions regarding technology acquisition, management, and application.

When your IT support person says something to you like "Your MTU size is too large, and you are getting significant packet fragmentation at the edge router", do you just glaze over? Well, most people would, so don't feel bad. I am certain there is jargon in your business that would make me glaze over as well. This book won't teach you to speak Geek, but it will try to give you enough information to get a gist of the technology. Personally, I don't speak Spanish, but I do understand baño, cerveza, burrito, and Policia. That is enough to get me by on a day trip to Tijuana, and I hope to do this for you as well. I don't mean I want to teach you to speak Spanish, but Geek. You know what I mean.

The rest of this book seeks to provide:

- An understanding of the types of IT support available to your business
- Some of the enabling technologies available to, and in use by, the large majority of businesses
- The technology and concepts that make up a good cyber-security posture
- Some basic IT management concepts that can help you in your business survive, grow, and thrive

If this sounds like information that could be useful, let's go on and get to it.

2 IT Support Models

"Imagine if every Thursday your shoes exploded if you tied them the usual way. This happens to us all the time with computers, and nobody thinks of complaining." - Jef Raskin

What this book is really all about, is how do you, as a non-technical business person, get your networks and computers to be a business tool, and not a productivity drain. That is the crux of it.

Unfortunately, we are long past the point where you simply plug a computer in and work on it, if a computer like that ever existed. The more connected the world becomes, the more dependent you become on the technology, the more you expect out of the technology, and the more it costs to correctly maintain. And make no mistake, it must be maintained!

There are many ways to go about this, I guess, but the big three are In-House, Break/Fix, and Managed Services. We will talk about the pluses and minuses of each in the coming pages.

Before we get to that, let me give you a word of warning: if your wife's aunt's church friend's nephew is "pretty good with computers", and is doing your support work for you, chances are you are not getting the right quality of service that you need, and your business might very well be at considerable risk.

Let's change the conversation a little bit, as a way of explanation. If your wife's aunt's church friend's nephew is "pretty good with math", are you going to get him to do your accounting? Or what if your wife's aunt's church friend's nephew is "pretty good with people", is he going to be doing your human resource work? I don't think so, at least not in my company. A well-run business has to consider IT just as much an essential part of the business as accounting, as human resources, as contracts, and as sales. To be blunt, those departments would cease to function if IT goes off the rails. A business that does not take IT seriously is simply a house built upon sand.

So, let's talk about the approaches that you can take to get the support your business needs.

In-House

What was once considered the standard way to support IT is to have your IT person in-house, and on the payroll. There is a convenience there that is undeniable. However, of the support models, this is the most expensive method for small businesses, by a long shot.

In smaller businesses, the IT person may often be that really good sales person who is also good with computers. Some of the time the salesperson is on the phone making sales and chasing leads and moving and shaking, creating revenue for the business, and earning his or her keep. The rest of the time, they are helping to solve computer trouble within the organization.

The staff loves it because they have someone at their beck and call. No matter what the salesperson is doing, the receptionist's problem with the printer becomes priority one. (By the way, it seems that no one ever thinks their computer problem is a low priority.)

This approach is slanted for convenience, but that convenience is expensive. It is nice to have someone there whenever you want them, without having to wait. It is also good to have someone there who knows your environment well. But you need to beware of these false benefits.

First off, when that salesperson is helping you reset your password for the fifth time, he is generating zero money for the business, and that holds true for most any position. Secondly, there is a friction loss in role change. If you got interrupted every couple of hours to go do something else, it would be hard to get anything done.

The Latin maxim writer Pubillus Syrus wrote, "To do two things at once is to do neither." That is very true in a case like this. Estimates range as high as 40% loss of efficiency when multi-tasking, so you could be paying much more than you should for similar work.

This isn't a good idea for the example salesperson, either. This person will find it difficult to hit sales targets, get promotions, raises, and bonuses, because they are up to 40% less efficient than their peers are. They are not likely to stay around for that and now you have lost a good technical person and a good salesperson in a single afternoon.

I know you might be thinking that your business is big enough to have a full-time IT person, so the salesperson can go back to selling. Maybe you are, but I don't think so. The reason I don't believe so is that a properly trained, properly tooled, properly compensated technician can support 100-200 computers without much trouble. If your business has 200 computers, you really are not the target audience of this book. Keep reading, though, because some of this will still apply to you.

So let's say you are 100-200 PCs and have your own technician, and life is good. Not so fast there, because your technician is missing something. What he is missing is a technical manager that tells them what to do, when to do it, how to do it, and verifies that it was completed accurately and on time. Since this book is targeted at non-technical business owners and managers, I think it is safe to say that you can't be the technical manager.

The lack of a technical manager is just the beginning. There is another issue afoot here. Your technician probably falls in one of two categories, complacent or driven. The complacent technician is going to hang around and continue to reinstall the word processors when they go south, and reboot the firewall when no one can get on the internet. What they won't do is drive your organization technically, keeping you up-to-date, or out in front of your competition. They have no management or internal peers to help them grow professionally, so they languish, and with them so goes your business.

Now you may believe you are lucky and have the driven technician, and perhaps you are. But then again…

The driven technician is going to be spending any free time reading and researching the latest technology, and getting a theoretical grasp of what is up and coming. For an engaged technician, that theoretical knowledge is like getting a picture of a glass of ice water on a summer day; it simply won't satisfy the thirst. Given that, the tech might try to convince you to make an investment in a technology that may or may not help your bottom line (the absolute measure of value), simply because they find it exciting, having lost their objectivity as to whether or not it provides business value. There is no technical manager to take that objective look and now you are left with disillusioning your superstar technician by turning down his request, or making an investment based on an emotional appeal. Not a good situation.

The superstar is going to want peer stimulation and challenge for professional growth. They are going to want what amounts to a research and development budget. They are going to want a career path. The only way for them to get that is to leave, and they will leave, just as soon as they find a dollar more an hour and the chance to play with some cool toys. It is how they are wired.

Now what? Try to hire another superstar only to keep them on for a year before they move on? Recruiting, hiring, and training are expensive. That is something you don't want to be doing every year or two.

Another thing you need to be aware of with the In-House Support approach, if you haven't thought about this before: like doctors, there are many different types of "computer people". There are generalists, which know a little about a lot, and are typically what you will hire internally in a small business. But a complete IT department is composed of technicians (generalists), database administrators, email administrators, network engineers, security engineers, and more. As a small business, it is hard to afford the complete suite of talent, but you really need those disciplines. Think about it like this: if you were diagnosed with cancer, you would likely seek out an Oncologist, not a General Practitioner.

For small businesses, the in-house support model is not really sustainable. At the extremes, you have a retired-in-place, technically-adequate employee, or you have a revolving door of top talent. Either way, this exposes the organization to a considerable amount of unnecessary risk.

Think about the things that your small business relies on to accomplish your mission; things that are not the mission itself like legal, accounting, and insurance. Now think about the mission. Are you a widget maker AND a law firm? Are you a bakery AND an accounting firm? No, you are probably not. There shouldn't be an AND in your business. It used to be that small businesses needed a banker, a lawyer, an accountant, and an insurance agent as partners to run their small business. Now you can add an IT provider to the list. Focus on the mission and outsource the rest, which makes for a nice segue…

Break/Fix

The first outsourced model of support is the traditional break/fix model. When something breaks, you call an IT provider, they come and fix it, and charge you by the hour. This same support model is used in many industries, such as appliance repair, plumbing, and so on.

This is a fairly simple model that provides the full range of IT talent that most businesses need. A typical break/fix provider will have trained technicians on staff that are dispatched when a call comes in. They arrive on site and take care of the problem.

The benefit of this model is that you, as a small business, can get access to a wide range of technical knowledge, talent, and support, but only have to pay for what you use. For most businesses that outsource their IT today, this is how it is done.

Subscribing to the old adage, "If it ain't broke, don't fix it." works well in many scenarios, and seems to make a lot of sense for IT. However, there are numerous of areas where this philosophy can be reckless, dangerous, and expensive.

Take our cars, for example. Most of us are good about getting regular oil changes to help avoid expensive engine rebuilds down the road. We are being proactive and taking steps to avoid potential disastrous consequences. Same thing with our health. We get regular medical and dental checkups to identify potential issues that can be addressed before a heart attack strikes, or oral surgery is necessary.

This should also be true with business IT systems. Businesses today rely heavily on their IT systems, and maintaining company IT infrastructure is obviously important. Access to line-of-business systems, such as sales and support tools, financial systems, and customer data is essential to your business success. If access to these systems is interrupted, there is direct impact to the bottom line, as staff may be idled while waiting for a repair, customers might not be getting the support they need, and vendors might not be getting paid. Tangible and intangible costs can add up in dollars and reputation.

In the break/fix model, you simply wait for something to break before taking any action. Take, for example, a failed hard disk in a critical system. When you or your staff determine you cannot access this system, you tinker with it for an hour or so trying to get it to boot back up. Failing that, you call your IT provider. Perhaps several hours later, a technician arrives on site to diagnose the problem, which takes an hour or so. Parts are ordered and within a day or two the technician returns, replaces the drive, and attempts to restore your lost data from a backup that has never been tested. Like the estimated 70% of of all tape backups, it fails. Now your staff has been idle for 2-3 days and your data is gone, and will have to be rebuilt manually.

This reactive maintenance model has the ability to have detrimental impact on a small business, and exposes the business to risk.

Another problem with the break/fix model is one of budgets and cash flow. Unless you can accurately predict what systems will break, when they will break, and what it will take to repair them, your IT budget is a crap shoot.

In small business, cash flow is king, and being unable to identify what your IT costs will be from week-to-week, month-to-month, and year-to-year induces financial risk that is unnecessary.

Another fundamental issue with the break/fix model is a lack of plans, goals, and consistency. Imagine your IT infrastructure is a new home, and your home builders work in the break/fix model. Each new contractor, from the block-layers to the trim carpenter, is called on site to install some feature, absent a set of plans. You are gong to wind up with frankenhouse. Without a clear plan, good documentation, and set goals, your IT infrastructure is doomed to fail, but luckily for the break/fix provider, there is money to be made off of you by holding it all together (for a while).

And there lies the single biggest issue I have with the break/fix model. The IT provider makes money when your systems are down and you aren't making money. It is an adversarial relationship at best, as the IT provider has no motivation to work fast or make permanent fixes. It is counter intuitive.

Your small business needs trusted advisors who have the same motivation for your business to succeed as you do. That is where Managed Services come in.

Managed Services

The easiest way to think of the Managed Service model is to think of a time-share condominium. With a time-share you get all of the benefits of having a vacation home, but you are only paying for what you use. Same for Managed Services. You get the technician, the network engineer, the security engineer, the technical manager, and the Chief Information Officer, but you only pay a small fraction of what all those things costs, independently. What is better is that the fractional cost is consistent and easy to budget. Essentially, you pay the same amount each month, and the Managed Service provider takes care of everything. This includes many things that the break/fix provider would not have been addressing, such as automatic application patching, anti-virus updates, and the reporting of those activities.

More so, the Managed Service provider takes a proactive role in monitoring and maintaining systems, making repairs, often before the end-user knows there is a problem.

Think back to the failed hard-disk scenario in the previous section. In the proactive Managed Services model, the scenario can be quite different.

As systems are monitored 24x7x365 for signs of poor performance or pending failure, the same failed drive scenario could go like this: the monitoring software on the server detects that a hard disk is showing signs of potential failure days or weeks in advance, even before you or your employees are aware of any issue. The Managed Service provider is automatically notified and remotely examines and diagnoses the issue. After business hours, the technician comes on-site to replace the drive, and then restores the data from a backup that the provider has regularly tested. The system is returned to fully operational status. The next day your employees return to work, never knowing that there was an issue. No down time, no impact, no lost revenue, no lost reputation.

As stated before, the proactive Managed Services model is generally a fixed-fee service. You pay a low, flat rate each month and enjoy complete managed care. Systems are monitored and maintained, around the clock, with proven tools and processes. Regular maintenance is performed, patches applied, firewalls monitored, backups tested, and viruses removed. No costly and unbudgeted emergency support bills.

Suffice it to say that when your IT systems are down, money is being lost. Even though it might be hard to quantify, taking a proactive approach to maintaining your IT systems is far less expensive than the reactive and potentially very costly nature of the break/fix model.

Along with proactive maintenance and fixed fees, many Managed Service offerings include a virtual Chief Information Officer, or vCIO. The role of the vCIO is to help you maximize the value of your IT spend.

The vCIO can help you create a technology roadmap that will identify the right technology at the right time to satisfy your business needs. This will make sure the server you buy today will work with your software tomorrow and vice versa. But mostly it puts you on a path whereby every technology decision has a place, a business purpose, a budget, and a high chance to be successful.

At first blush, the Managed Services model may give the appearance of being more expensive than break/fix, and to a degree it has to be. There is simply more work to be done; work that was not previously being done. However, just because it wasn't being done in no way diminishes the need for it to be done. Just like a car, computer systems and networks need regular monitoring and maintenance to avoid expensive and catastrophic failures. You don't have to change the oil in your car, but sooner or later your engine will blow. Same principle with computers. What the perceived higher cost does, is smooth out the emergency expenditures, and potential lost revenue.

The Managed Service model affords your small business the opportunity to compete on a leveled playing field with your larger, more well-funded, competitors. It provides the necessary maintenance and monitoring to help reduce the chance of catastrophic outages that can greatly impact business. It does this in a disciplined fashion, at a fixed price, and greatly reduces financial risk to your small business.

The Path to Managed Services

Many small businesses will work their way through your wife's aunt's church friend's nephew who is "pretty good with computers" and on to the break/fix model. Along the way they may even flirt with "block hours" (a break/fix model that allows you to buy a recurring block of break/fix labor at slightly discounted rates.)

Those small businesses that are poised for growth, however, will likely embrace the Managed Services concept. This concept has been around a while, and is suitable for businesses large and small. I worked at a very, very large Department of Defense company in the 90's when the company moved to Managed Services and transferred all IT support, including the ownership of the company computers, to a large Managed Services firm. Some years later, the U. S. Navy did the same thing. Why? Because Managed Services is a model that works.

My advice to you, as a small business owner or manager, is to focus on what you are good at, and leave lawyering to the lawyers, the accounting to the accountants, the IT to the geeks.

3 Choosing an IT Service Provider

"In a few minutes a computer can make a mistake so great that it would have taken many men many months to equal it." - Anonymous

Choosing a computer support company isn't easy. There is no shortage of horror stories about incompetent computer repair "gurus" bungling jobs and causing more problems as a result of their loose morals or gross incompetence. I'm sure if you talk to your own friends and colleagues you will get an earful of the unfortunate experiences they have encountered in this area.

Why is this? Because the computer repair and consulting industry, along with a lot of other industries, has its own share of incompetent or unethical businesses that will try to take advantage of trusting business owners who simply do not have the ability to determine whether or not the technician knows what they are doing. Sometimes this is out of greed for your money, but more often, it's simply because they don't have the skills and competency to do the job right, but won't tell you that up front. Instead they provide misleading information and unqualified technicians, as well as poor management and terrible customer service.

Here's an embarrassing (and little-known) fact about the IT support industry: it is not regulated like many other professional service industries, which means anyone can claim they are a "computer repair expert." In fact, a lot of the businesses in this industry started because the owner was fired or laid off from their job and couldn't find work anywhere else. This means many of the so-called experts are useless and make sleazy auto repair shops look like the pinnacle of virtue and competence.

Electricians, plumbers, lawyers, realtors, dentists, doctors, accountants, etc., are heavily regulated to protect the consumer from receiving substandard work or getting ripped off. However, the computer industry is still highly unregulated and there aren't any laws in existence to protect the consumer.

Anyone who can hang out a shingle can promote themselves as a computer expert. Even if they are honestly trying to do a good job for you, their inexperience can cost you dearly in your network's speed and performance or in lost or corrupt data files.

The rest of this chapter will provide you with many of the key elements you should be looking for when trying to select an IT service provider.

Customer Service

When it comes to the best service providers, they will have a lot of things in common. They will be responsive, courteous, reliable, and goal oriented, but more is required.

- Better IT service providers will answer their support lines live, with a qualified technician, as well as provide a mechanism for after-hours support. Why? First, it is important to have someone working on your problem as soon as possible, and second because many small business owners and staff often work outside normal hours. If they cannot access their computer network and can't get hold of anyone to help them, it's incredibly frustrating.

- A qualified IT service provider will guarantee to have a technician working on a problem within a specified timeframe, preferably within 60 minutes or less of your call. Down time is lost revenue, and a good service provider should be conscious of this.

- Technicians should be trained to speak in common language when discussing technical problems with clients. Make sure your IT service provider will take the time to explain both the problem and resolutions in terms that you can understand, not Geek-speak.

- Your service provider should not only be willing, but should insist on conducting quarterly review meetings with you to look for new ways to help improve your operations, lower costs, increase efficiencies, and resolve any problems that may be arising.

- Detailed invoices that show what work was done, why and when, are essential in the customer satisfaction. Make sure your provider can and will provide this information, so you never have to guess what you are paying for.

- Here's something to consider: if your provider causes a problem with your network that causes you to be down for hours or days or to lose data, who's responsible? Here's another question to consider: if one of their technicians gets hurt at your office, who's paying? Make sure your provider carries both Errors and Omissions (E&O) insurance, as well as Workman's Comp.

- A good IT provider should be able to perform project work that is fixed-priced and guaranteed to be completed on time, in writing. This is important because many unethical or incompetent computer guys will only quote "time and materials", which gives them free rein to nickel-and-dime you as well as take as much time as they want on completing a project.

Practices and Procedures

Make sure that your chosen IT vendor's practices are in keeping with industry best practices and good common sense. There should be continued monitoring, maintenance, and reporting, and the terms of their agreement should be clear.

- A qualified IT service provider should be willing and able to remotely monitor your network 24x7 to keep critical security settings, virus definitions, and security patches up-to-date and prevent problems from turning into downtime, viruses, lost data, and other issues. Your network should be constantly reviewed for developing problems, security issues, and other problems so they can be addressed before they turn into bigger problems.
- Make sure your provider can provide you with monthly or weekly detailed reports that shows an overall health score of your network and the updates to your anti-virus, security settings, patches and other important network checks (like hard-drive space, backups, speed and performance, etc.).
- Make sure it is standard procedure for them to provide you with written network documentation detailing critical passwords, user information, hardware inventory, etc. You should never have to ask an IT company for that documentation. If you get the sneaking suspicion that your current IT person is keeping this under their control as a means of job security, get rid of them. This is downright unethical and dangerous to your organization, so don't tolerate it!

- Make sure you understand what the IT vendor's package support really includes. Are there "gotchas" hidden in the fine print? One of the more popular service plans offered by consulting firms today is an "all-inclusive" or "all-you-can-eat" managed services plan. These are actually a good thing because they'll save you a lot of money in the long run. However, make sure you really understand what is and isn't included. Some things to consider are:
  - Is phone/e-mail help desk included or extra?
  - What about network upgrades, moves, or adding/removing users?
  - Is hardware and/or software included?
  - What about 3rd-party software support?
  - What are the costs/consequences of early cancellation?
  - What if you aren't happy with their services? Do they offer a money-back guarantee?
  - If the hardware and software is included, what happens if you cancel the contract?
  - Are off-site backups included? To what degree?
  - If you have a major disaster, is restoring your network included or extra?
  - What about on-site support calls? Or support to remote offices?
  - Are home PCs used to access the company's network after hours included or extra?

There is so much variation in offerings that no two packages might be the same. In most cases, it is not the dishonest vendor trying to deceive you, but the honest vendor trying to define clear contractual edges to prevent abuse and contractual over-exposure. Ask your vendor to describe in detail what is being covered before you sign any agreement.

Backups and Disaster Recovery

It is not a question of if disaster will strike, but *when*. That disaster may be when a fire guts your office, a hard disk fails and data is lost, or simply a user deleting an important file. A good IT provider will make sure you are taking the right steps to protect yourself.

- An IT service provider should insist on monitoring an off-site, as well as an on-site, disk-based backup, and they should not allow your business to depend on tape backup systems, due to the extremely high failure rate.
- Your provider should insist on doing periodic test restores of your backups, or employ an automatic method of verification, to make sure the data is not corrupt and could be restored in the event of a disaster.
- Make sure your selected IT provider will work with you to create a simple written disaster recovery plan for your data and network.

Technical Expertise and Support

As mentioned before, a good IT support vendor will have a live help desk. However, it is not good enough to simply have a warm body answer the phone.

- Make sure your vendor's help desk (also known as a Service Desk) is staffed live, and is US-based (assuming you are in the US, that is). Ask if you can listen in on a couple of calls to make sure the staff is helpful and friendly.
- Ask what, if any, certifications that their technicians maintain. Make sure their techs are not learning on your time and your dime.
- Make sure they are familiar with your unique line-of-business applications. They should own the problems

24

with all line-of-business applications for you. That doesn't mean they can fix faulty software – but they should be the liaison between you and your vendor to resolve problems you are having and make sure these applications work smoothly for you.

- When something goes wrong with your Internet service, phone systems, printers or other IT services, your IT service provider should own the problem, interfacing with other IT providers, so you don't have to try and resolve any of these issues on your own – that's just plain old good service and something many computer guys won't do.

Mistakes to Avoid

Choosing a computer consultant based on a single phone call is a mistake. I know you get frustrated and want to throw that device out the window. The first person you get on the phone wins. Try to hold off. Invite them into your office and ask them for a written proposal. Be clear on what your expectations are and what type of problems you want them to resolve. A competent professional should offer to do an audit of your network to audit and diagnose your systems before quoting you anything. After all, would you take a doctor's word that you need surgery if they hadn't done x-rays or other diagnostics? Of course not! Prescription without diagnosis is malpractice.

Don't choose a computer consultant that doesn't have a written guarantee of service. A good consulting firm should be accountable for their services and for fixing things right. If you aren't pleased with a job that was done, they should (at a minimum) make it right for free; and if they simply cannot resolve an issue to your satisfaction, you shouldn't get stuck with the bill.

Plus, the fact that they stand behind their work with a guarantee shows they have confidence in themselves to make you a happy client. And don't fall for the "We don't offer one because people will take advantage of us" routine. Most people just want an honest service at a reasonable price. If you give them that, they are happy to pay. Are there a few unethical folks out there? Of course, but they are the minority.

Ask for references! Don't just take the sales guy's word that they are good – ask to speak to a client. If they hesitate or cannot provide you with references, don't trust them!

Choosing a computer consultant who cannot remotely monitor, update, and support your network shows a lack of ability. In this day and age, a computer consultant who doesn't do this is living in the Stone Age. You want someone to do this because it will dramatically increase your network's security and will enable them to do faster repairs. That's not to say they shouldn't come on site; but remote monitoring and repairs make fixing problems faster for you and help avoid problems cropping up in the first place.

Don't choose an IT provider who is willing to give you a quote for network support over the phone. Just like a good doctor, an honest and professional technician will need to diagnose your network before they can quote any price over the phone. Without at least looking at you network, how can they have a good idea as to what is wrong?

Also, some vendors will quote you a cheap rate over the phone to get in the door, but then jack up the prices once they get in your office by taking 3 times as long, selling you add-ons and up-sells, etc. And finally, reputable firms don't charge by the hour anyway – they give you a fixed, flat rate. If they know what they are doing, then they should know what it costs.

There are plenty of good IT firms out there, and I encourage you to find the right one. Armed with these tips and the information contained in the rest of this book, you should be able to do just that.

4 Enabling Technology

"Once a new technology rolls over you, if you're not part of the steamroller, you're part of the road." – Stewart Brand

There are so many new technologies and techniques coming out every day it's hard to keep up with them, even for me, someone for who keeping up with these things is part of my job description. This chapter will explore some of the technologies I think can have an impact on your business and bears a little exploration. We will even talk about some old technology (backups) that has changed significantly enough to be considered emerging again. Read on.

Virtualization

Back in the day, good server management meant dedicating a server to every line-of-business application. E-mail had its own server, accounting had its own server, ERP had its own server and so on. Small businesses could easily have 5-10 servers to cover the day-to-day business needs. This separation was necessary due to survivability concerns. If e-mail was down, you still want to be able to sell product. If the ERP system needed maintenance, you still want to be able to pay and get paid.

Unfortunately, that segregated approach often left expensive servers with an average utilization of less than 5%. Oh, and did I mention that servers are expensive?

As time has passed, servers have become more and more powerful, reliable, redundant, and again, expensive. This means, on a well-equipped server you could lose a disk drive and replace it, losing no data, and without even rebooting the machine. The power supply might fail, but no worries, you have another. Same with network cards and so on. These are essential capabilities for a server that is running your business, but they are still only using less than 5% of the available capacity.

So what if you could share the remaining 95% of the resources with your other servers and line-of-business applications? Well, you can. That is where virtualization comes in.

Virtualization is accomplished by having specialized software pretend to be hardware. Each piece of your server, such as disk drives, internet connections, and even the keyboard, mouse, and monitor, becomes a piece of software – simply files stored on the server. This pretend hardware is called a virtual server.

Think about it this way, if you took a camera and snapped a picture of your dog, the image of your dog becomes a file on your computer. If you look at the image, you immediately recognize it as Spot. If your friends want to see Spot, you can make a copy of the file and send it to them. It is still not a dog, but everyone recognizes what is in the picture is a real dog: Spot.

As it goes with dogs, so goes it with virtualized servers. A virtualized machine is simply one that has been converted into files. It can be copied, moved, modified, and deleted, just like your photo of Spot. However, we want to bring these files to life so everyone can have a dog, err.... server.

This little magic is done using a special piece of software called a hypervisor. Some hypervisor names you may have heard of are VMWare, Hyper-V, and Virtual Box, but don't worry about the names, as they all do the same thing.

A hypervisor is a special operating system, like Windows or Unix, that is installed directly onto your server. It completely replaces any other operating system that might have been there before. Your server is now referred to as the "host system". The host system controls all of the resources of the physical server and will manage them as necessary for the "guest systems".

Guest systems are those virtual servers that have been created with the hypervisor software and are pretending to be actual servers. These guest systems exist in a many-to-one relationship with the host system. So, for example, each of your servers, from accounting to ERP, from e-mail to document management, can be guest systems of a single hypervisor (or host system), each taking up a small percentage of server resources, and therefore achieving better server utilization. More bang for your buck, if you will.

Certainly you can't achieve perfect utilization in a virtualized server environment, but you can still get a lot of benefit. As an example, if you bought five physical servers at $3,000 each, you are out $15,000. However, if you bought a single server capable of running all of your virtualized servers, perhaps with more memory, disk, and processing power, plus the hypervisor software, you might be out $7,500. Now, all of the guest servers run from a single physical server, but unless you went in the computer room to look for the servers themselves, you would never be able to tell. You will still have all of the functionality and performance of the much more expensive multi-server configuration, at half the price. And there are other ways to save money with virtualization as well.

First up on the savings list is the consumption of electrical and cooling. Big servers draw a lot of electricity and generate heat. Multiply that out by the number of servers you have and you can see that the electrical and cooling costs (one and the same) can become substantial. Virtualization can save you a lot in this area.

Next item is that most line-of-business applications will periodically have to be upgraded, and often, that upgrade breaks the application, resulting in significant downtime. Virtualization reduces risk here in a couple of ways. You can simply make a moment-in-time snapshot (or copy) of your virtualized server before the upgrade begins. If patching the machine fails, you can roll back to the snapshot of how your machine looked before you mangled it, and all is right with the world. Downtime is minimized and you are back to making money again.

Another approach to the same situation is to make a complete copy of the machine, which is as simple as a few mouse clicks. Once you have done that, you apply the patch or upgrade to the copied machine and test it in a safe environment. If it all checks out, you roll the change into production and march on. No downtime, no lost revenue.

Also, since all of the virtual servers are simply a collection of files, entire servers can be backed up or even copied to new hypervisors on new physical servers. If your server is getting a little long in the tooth and you need to replace it, all you need to do is purchase a new physical server, install your hypervisor of choice, and one evening after work, copy all of your servers over from the old host machine. The next morning the whole company will be remarking about how fast their systems seem today, without ever knowing there was a hardware change.

In more complex virtualized environments, the ability to avoid impact due to hardware failure is even more advanced. In those environments where there are groups of host systems, you can move a guest system to a new host system without any interruption of service; even with users still logged on and working.

There are so many benefits to virtualization that I advocate it even if you only have only one server. In that scenario, configure your hardware as a virtualized host with a single guest operating system running your line-of-business application. Virtualization has so much utility, I consider it essential to well-run system.

Don't try this at home, kids, as implementing a virtualized environment is a task that is complex. Get some professional help from someone who has done it. It will be money well spent.

Telework

Telework, or telecommuting, or remote work, or whatever you want to call it, can be a fantastic option for some small businesses, at the same time being completely unsuitable for others. While I will touch on some lessons learned later, let's talk about the enabling technologies.

There are a couple of ways to accomplish telework that I will talk about, whether by allowing a remote computer to connect to the network via a Virtual Private Network (VPN) or by connecting to specific internal applications via a website or web portal. (Geeks love the word portal, for some reason.) There are reasons to support the use of either, and I will try to address them here.

A VPN is a direct link to your network from some less secure place, such as your employee's home or the local coffee shop. Generally, the remote PC (the one your employee has) uses an encryption language over a standard internet connection that provides secure communication to your internal network, and typically exposes everything on the internal network, such as servers and applications, to the user. This is the most powerful of the two telework scenarios we will discuss, but also has the greatest amount of risk.

When the user logs in, his machine will behave just as it would if he had walked in the office and plugged it in the wall. This is all well and good as long as the user maintains positive control of the PC, the PC is patched and running anti-virus, and obeys all of your IT guidance. The traditional VPN, however, is more difficult to configure, manage, and maintain than the alternative. In my experience, this approach is well suited only for devices, such as laptops, owned and maintained by the company and in the possession of an employee that has some measure of technical aptitude.

If you just want your users to be able to do their time sheets from home on their own computer, or some similar situation, I would recommend the web portal approach. You wouldn't want to expose your time keeping server to the whole internet, and should restrict it only to your employees. In this situation, a web portal approach is better suited. The user goes to a URL such as https://portal.yourcompany.biz and logs in to the web portal. Depending on the user, they may see one or more application icons that they have been given permission to see, such as Time Keeping and the ERP system. By clicking on the application icon, the application is launched in the browser window without exposing the internal network to whatever evil might be lurking in the user's computer. Another benefit of this type of remote work, is that every interaction is centrally logged. More on that in a minute.

Before you choose to implement a telework scenario for your business, you need to make sure the business is suitable for it. If you own a KFC franchise, it is not going to work as you can't yet remotely fry chicken. However, if you run a data entry shop, this might just be the ticket.

If you do choose to go the telework route, you have to make sure that the role is appropriate and the employees you give access to it are worthy.

As for suitable roles, your receptionist can't work from home unless your office is in their house. It doesn't matter who or how good the receptionist is, the job of receptionist requires someone to be there to answer the door and deliver the mail. Conversely, accounting may very well be a good fit for teleworking.

As for the individual, some employees can be more productive from home, or the beach, or a cabin, than they can at the office. They love their job, they have a sense of commitment, they are achievers. They can be trusted to hit their goals and have discipline to get the job done. Others simply cannot.

My experience shows that often, the phrase "I am going to work from home for the rest of the day" means "I am going home, I am going to login to the VPN so it looks like I am working, and then I am going to watch Ellen for the rest of the day because I am unhappy here."

This is where the logs come in. Any good VPN system should be equipped with central logging features. Use the logs to monitor the user activity on a regular basis and pull the plug on the abusers. It will happen, trust me.

The telework concept can be good, though. The overachievers will take the opportunity to work from anywhere. Employees with sick children can stay home and still get work done, and inclement weather, such as a blizzard or flooded streets, has less of an impact on productivity.

Telework can even be used to cut costs. A well-functioning company can have a virtual office with everyone working remotely. You can meet in-person once a week, talk by phone often, and get the job done. This can save money in rent, utilities, and insurance. This certainly can't work for everyone, but some form of it might work for you and your business.

Backup Technology

I would bet you don't think of backups as really cool stuff, but if you will read all the way through this section, you will find some new backup technologies that can strengthen your business in multiple ways. Backups have been around since data was born, but this essential technology must be part of every serious business infrastructure.

Backup Strategy

Although some small businesses might not think so, having a good backup is essential. So essential, in fact, that 90% of small businesses that suffer a catastrophic data loss are out of business within a year. That is a big deal.

Think about it. If you lost all of your customer information, patient records, employee records, or accounting data, how would you recover from that? In most cases, you couldn't. Game over. Thanks for playing.

So it just makes good sense to have a backup strategy. Yes, a strategy, not just a tape drive, and a strategy that includes how often you back it up (Recovery Point Objective) and how quickly you need to recover it (Recovery Time Objective). Let's explore these nerd phrases a little more.

First, let's look at Recovery Point Objectives (RPO). Imagine that you are a financial advisor using mostly online tools, and generating 2 or 3 documents each day that are stored on your local file server. Losing a day's worth of documents is only a minor setback, but a week's worth would cost you quite a bit in labor and lost sales opportunities trying to recreate them from scratch. In this scenario, backing them up once a day makes more sense than once a week. And backing them up once an hour is overkill, simply because they don't change that often. In this scenario, your RPO of 24 hours is a nice balance, and in my experience, the most common routine among those doing backups.

Now imagine you are a sales organization with a staff of 20 sales people taking phone orders all day, and those orders are entered into your fulfillment system. Can you afford to lose all of your sales records for a week? A day? An hour? Were it my business, an RPO of 1 hour is the appropriate interval. In this scenario, all of the sales orders are backed up each hour throughout the work day. If disaster happens, a server crashes, or your building catches fire, you have lost only a maximum of one hour's worth of sales data.

The next question is how much history do you need? Do you want to get back to the original version of the spreadsheet that you created last year? Or do you believe that if you haven't touched it in a month, you'll never need it again? This needs to be factored into your strategy.

You may be thinking why not just back up everything every hour and keep it forever, regardless of which of these scenarios is appropriate? Well, backup media (disk, tape, etc.) and network capacity are limited resources with associated costs that must be considered in determining your RPO. You don't want to have to buy the largest backup device to hold everything you want to backup every hour, forever, if you don't need that kind of coverage. Nor do you want to slow your network to a crawl every hour while your staff is trying to get work done.

Consider also that backup systems typically provide file versioning. Meaning, if you change a file once an hour (say a spreadsheet), and you back it up once an hour, you have 8 copies of that file for a single day. Multiply this out over the week, month, or year, and it becomes a significant number of versions, and adds to your growing storage requirements. RPO is a tradeoff. You should talk to your IT provider about the best RPO for your organization.

Now let's address Recovery Time Objectives (RTO). How quickly do you need your data to be restored in the event of a loss? I am sure you are thinking "immediately", but while we can get much closer to that these days, more so than ever before, that just isn't the reality. So, do you need the data back in a hour, a day, or a week? These decisions help to determine what technology to put in place, and what price you are going to pay.

If you have identified an RTO of an hour, for example, you will need to have local backup storage that is disk-based, not tape. If an RTO of a week is fine with you, then cloud-only storage might be more appropriate. (See the next section on cloud computing.) These choices are going to impact cost.

Again, like RPO, RTO is a negotiation.

Backup Procedures

With RPO and RTO out of the way, we need to talk about a couple of fundamental concepts regarding backups, specifically testing and off-site storage.

In some form or fashion, you need to test your backups at least once a month. No exceptions. While backups have become more reliable over the years, they are not perfect, and some backups are far less perfect than others. If you are not testing your backups, then you don't have a backup. What you have is a chance at a backup, and in some cases, not a very good chance.

Each month, at a minimum, you should randomly pick a file, folder, or even a whole machine, and restore it from the backup media to some alternate location (please do not overwrite your live data). If everything works as expected, great. If not, it's time to find out why. When your systems are down hard and your employees are idle is not the time to troubleshoot a backup or find out your data is gone.

You need to store copies of your backups in an off-site location, away from the servers you are backing up. What good is a backup of your server if the server and the backup were lost in a fire? Zilch.

Make a backup according to your RPO and RTO and make sure a copy of the media is moved off site at least weekly, leaving a copy on site as well. Make it part of the business process, have someone accountable for it, and someone else to measure it. Make it routine.

Backup Types

So let's move on to the types of backups you could implement, first of which is called file and folder backup. Just like it sounds, it backs up files and folders. This has been around a long time, and if you are in any way familiar with backup systems, this is likely the one that you know. The backup software simply runs down the list of files and folders you tell it to back up and writes it out to the backup device. In a lot of cases, this might include the operating system files, not just documents and databases, allowing a machine to be rebuilt on a new piece of hardware. With file and folder backups you can backup and restore as little as a single file to as much as the whole machine, and anything in between.

File and folder backups have worked well for quite some time, but there is a new sheriff in town. The new sheriff is image-based backup. Like file and folder backup, image-based backup includes all of your documents as well as operating system files. Like file and folder backup, you can restore a single file, a previous version of the file, or the whole machine. Where image-based backups go "all Buzz Lightyear" on you is that they create a perfect functioning image of your server that can be started as a virtual machine on the backup server in seconds, replacing a failed machine, and getting you back in business. (Read the previous section on virtualization.)

So think about this in terms of Recovery Time Objective. Your business is humming along creating sales calls and moving product. All of a sudden, the power goes *blip* momentarily and down goes the ERP system. Unfortunately, the server won't boot back up. No more order taking, no more customer support. (Side note: someone should have tested your UPS system, but that is another topic.)

In minutes, and in some cases, seconds, assuming you are using an image-based backup system, a perfect copy of your ERP server can be brought online and business can continue, likely before the sales staff gets back from the break room.

What makes image-based backups even more awesome, is the ability to start the server in a remote data center. Imagine that the *blip* that got your ERP system was a tornado that ripped the roof off your building. Luckily, no one was hurt, but now, how are you going to do business without a building and your servers? This is not a problem with an image-based system. Most image-based backup offerings have a cloud component where you can, in just a few hours, boot your systems securely in the cloud, allowing your employees to access them from wherever they have an internet connection. This could easily be the difference between being in business and being out of business.

Backup Media

While there are multiple variations in backup solutions, we need to scope this discussion with generalities. I am certain, if you look hard enough, you can find a device or technology that defies what I have said and will say. That would make backups a book all unto itself, so for now, let's talk in generic terms.

Tape Backup

For you smug readers out there thinking "I already have a tape backup system in place and we carry the tapes home every day", wipe that smile off your face. There is a problem here that you need to be aware of. (Unfortunately, you probably stopped reading this section a long time ago, but you really need to hear this message.)

Tape had its day. It was the standard for data backup. That day has passed.

Tape backups fail. Some estimates say that 100% of tape backups will fail, and given time, I know that is true. However, I think the real number, based on my experience, is more in the neighborhood of 70%. That is huge. If the brakes on your car failed 70% of the time, you wouldn't be alive to read this book, or if you were, you would be sitting in the lobby down at Budget Brakes while doing so.

The problem with tape is that it wears and stretches, and the drives get out of alignment. This can cause tapes to be completely unreadable, or just unreadable on drives except the one that wrote it.

Another issue with tape is that you may not be able to find a compatible replacement tape drive (one that can read your existing backups) when your current drive fails. Manufacturers are always changing or retiring models. This could leave you searching through EBay trying to find something to read your files, while your sales staff sits idle.

Now think of your RTO. Tape is a serial media, meaning that one file is written right after the other, all along the tape. If the one file you want is at the far end of the tape, you have to read through the whole tape to get to the end to restore it, and if the next file is at the beginning, you have to go the other way. Tape is slow and time is money.

Disk-Based Backup

Far superior to tape backup is disk-based backup. Disk-based backup is faster, more dependable, and more portable. Typical disk-based systems are attached to your system directly or over the network, and each has its benefits.

A directly connected system usually does not use any network bandwidth, and therefore does not have a major impact on network users. They are typically faster than network systems due to the limitations of the network itself, and they are generally easily removed for off-site storage. They are also easy to lose or damage, and typically only support a single machine at a time.

A network-based system is still quite fast when compared to tape, and can be optimized to have little impact on the network. It is highly reliable, and can be configured to migrate your data to a secure off-site location automatically. No more worrying about where the admin placed the tape, or who now has access to your data if the tape was somehow lost or stolen.

Also, this style of backup system is what enables the image-based local and off-site virtualization discussed in the previous section.

If you only take one piece of advice from this book, heed this. Get off of tape as a backup media. It is a road to ruin.

Cloud Computing

A few years ago, all of a sudden, and without warning, everything was cloud this and cloud that. And most people were awed or wowed or confused. Surprisingly enough, it really wasn't anything new. With a little technology update, some repackaging and rebranding, "Cloud" became the thing.

Let me draw you a mental image of cloud computing, before we go much further. Imagine that e-mail server in your computer room there at your office. Now imagine that e-mail server in a computer room somewhere in New Jersey with a thousand-mile-long network cable connected between it and your office. Voila'. Cloud computing. Everything essentially works just the same. While there is far more to it than that, it doesn't have to be intimidating.

Cloud computing is sort of like a stool with three legs. Those legs are Infrastructure-as-a-Service (IaaS), Software-as-a-Service (SaaS), and Platform-as-a-Service (PaaS). For the purpose of this book, we won't be covering PaaS, as it is targeted for a more technical audience. However, we will go into SaaS and IaaS a little deeper to see why you might want to implement them in your business.

Software-as-a-Service

We will start with Software-as-a-Service, or SaaS, as you are probably more familiar with it. Do you have a Gmail, Hotmail, or Yahoo email account? If so, you are already using SaaS. These companies have email servers set up in the cloud, of which you enjoy the benefits. The software on these machines is provided to you "as a service". Easy, peasy, lemon-squeezy.

Now let's take that one step further. Microsoft Exchange is arguably the most powerful email server on the planet, and it is also probably the most difficult to manage and maintain. Businesses running an Exchange server in-house need good technical talent on staff to keep it running smoothly and get it back up and running when, and I do mean when, it goes in the tank. Multiple companies now offer Exchange in the cloud, including Microsoft themselves. These companies have the extensive talent on board to implement, monitor, and maintain an Exchange server for you for just a few dollars a month. This keeps you from having to buy a server, buy the software, hire the technician, perform the backups, etc. A small business can gain great competitive advantage by moving to a cloud email server.

If your small business wants to dip its toe into the cloud computing pool, this is the single best place to start. If you are currently managing a mail server in-house, you will someday thank me for that advice.

These days, there are more and more applications available in the cloud. When I started my latest company, I had the opportunity to retool my line-of-business applications. The first evaluation criteria for any line-of-business application was its availability in the cloud. Unless the application is unsuitable for the cloud (more on that later) I *insist* on it being in the cloud, and I'm an IT person, for cripes sake.

SaaS applications are generally sold on a subscription basis with low-to-no startup costs or capital investments. These subscription services keep your software patched and up to date. All you have to do is use it and pay for it.

Sure, there are some tradeoffs, usually in the form of lack of customizations, but those tradeoffs are generally not that impactful. For example, if you use a widget on your local Exchange server that adds a legal disclaimer message to the end of your email, it won't work on a SaaS email solution, because then every other user on that email service would have to use it. Likely, your SaaS provider has a different tool to provide the same or similar service, in a more generic fashion. Often a slight modification to business practice can overcome the shortcomings and limitations of SaaS.

Infrastructure-as-a-Service

Infrastructure-as-a-Service, or IaaS, is the other part of cloud computing that stands to really impact your small business, but it is not a panacea.

In the IaaS model, cloud providers, such as Amazon, Google, and Microsoft, provide you the ability to run your virtual servers from their computer rooms on their hardware. If you think back to the section of this book on virtualization, you will remember that one physical host machine can run multiple guest machines. That is what enables these cloud providers to provide these infrastructure services. They pool hundreds of physical servers together using virtualization software, and allow you to rent a slice of it. In most cases you can migrate your servers over from your location, or rebuild them from scratch in the cloud. You rent the amount of memory, disk space, and processing power you need, connect using a Virtual Private Network (see the previous telework discussion) and get back to work, just with your server or servers in a different location.

You don't have to buy or maintain hardware, but you do have to work within the security constraints and resource allocations that all other tenants of this environment have to abide by. This is considered the public cloud and it caters to the lowest common denominator for configuration. This is not necessarily a bad thing. I would dare say that most users of the cloud are in the public cloud.

However, if your application must have very specific security and compliance, for example, then the private cloud is likely more suitable for you. Within the private cloud, entire resource pools and physical servers are dedicated to your environment, and are highly configurable to your needs. For example, financial institutions must comply with the security controls set forth in the Sarbanes-Oxley act. This is an onerous regulation to force on everyone in the public cloud, so a private cloud is better suited. Private clouds can be hosted with a public cloud provider, in a server room co-location facility, or even in your own organization. If you haven't figured it out by now, the private cloud is going to be more expensive.

Many organizations will fall into the hybrid cloud model, where some application require a very specific environment and others do not. The hybrid model is simply the use of both public and private clouds.

From a maintenance responsibility standpoint, in the public cloud, the cloud provider is responsible for maintenance, whereas in the private cloud, your business would have the responsibility. In the hybrid cloud, the maintenance is split accordingly.

Why or Why Not Move to the Cloud

So with all the tradeoffs, why move anything at all to the cloud? There are great advantages to moving applications to the cloud, and the first of which is the ability of the application to remain up and available to end users, at a near constant level. The sheer amount of redundancy, specialized implementations, specific technical talent, consistent proactive maintenance and monitoring provided by a cloud provider, means greater uptime and productivity.

Cloud computing also has the benefit of a more predictable IT budget, without a large capital outlay for hardware and software acquisition. This is a very appealing concept for a money-conscious small business.

Lastly, at least for this book, is scalability. Let's say your business sells fireworks online, and your webserver is hosted in the public cloud. In the month leading up to the 4th of July and the month leading up to New Year's eve, your servers are slammed, but ten months of the year they barely bump off idle. In the cloud, you can simply add extra memory and processors for June and December, and take them away for the rest of the year, saving a few bucks. Brilliant.

So then, why not move everything to the cloud? Well, some things don't work well in the cloud, particularly those things that are either compute-intensive or generate large amounts of network traffic.

For example, if your line-of-business application is a math modeling application that uses tons of processor resources to produce computational models, this will cause resource competition with the other hosted applications and performance will suffer.

Another ill-fitting scenario might be if you are a video editor reading and writing huge video files to and from the file server all the time. If that file server is in the cloud, the network will be punished and you will get bored waiting. In both cases, the math application or the video file server, it would be better to host them locally.

One last reason not to move to the cloud: If you are in Badger Breath, Wisconsin, and a DSL connection is the fastest internet available, the cloud, in most any form, is going to be painfully slow. I would recommend that any business looking to make a cloud push get business-class internet. A business needs business-class services anyway. That's why they call them business-class services.

Social Media

Social media is likely one of the more game changing technologies to come along in a while. This new media has global reach, a huge audience, little-to-no entry fee, and near instantaneous interaction. Consider that the juggernaut Facebook is reporting 1.44 billion (with a B) active users in 2015. That doesn't count for Instagram, Pinterest, LinkedIn, YouTube, and the myriad of other social media platforms. With that many users, it only makes sense that businesses, large and small, are trying to find ways to leverage these platforms to build brand image, engage existing customers, and recruit new ones, and engage your employees.

Engage Your Customers

With so many social media platforms to choose from, it is unadvisable for a small business to try to employ them all, as it has the ability to dilute your message. So here is the simple test that will guide you toward your choice or choices: What social media platform do your customers use?

On the one hand, if your business creates and sells "Turnip Tot" dolls, then LinkedIn, the professional business platform, is not going to have the customers you are looking for. You are likely going to be looking for the mothers of young children, so perhaps consider Facebook or Pinterest for your campaigns.

On the other hand, if you are a consulting firm or business coach, Facebook is not the place. LinkedIn is where you should be, because business people, including executive-level officers, are there.

If you are in the service industry, let's say air conditioning repair, perhaps YouTube is the place to be. You could build out a series of videos on how to do routine maintenance on heating and air systems without exposing your secret sauce. When the do-it-yourselfer who follows your channel needs real help, you will be top of mind. You are building your brand image: a company that wants to help the little guy, without charging $100 an hour to change an air filter.

In the same sense of building brand image, these social media platforms differ from traditional print, radio, and television. A typical commercial is not the most well received on social media platforms. Sure CNN.com drops a Verizon commercial on you before every video, but news sites aren't social (despite the despised comment section at the bottom of each page).

It is more desirous to provide information that is useful to the reader, and start a conversation. The business coach may want to write an article about sales techniques that engage the reader. The "Turnip Tot" maker might want publish the birth story of "Rudy Behga", their most popular doll.

Make your social media content interesting, not a sales pitch. Be authentic. As the old saying goes, people want to buy, not be sold. Make it consistent. A regular weekly or monthly post may have greater impact than a daily SPAM blast, and it is easier to create good content less frequently.

If you choose to use social media as a customer engagement platform, I would recommend you read one of the 70,000+ titles available on Amazon.com regarding this topic. Just search on "social media for business".

Engage Your Employees

Customers and potential customers are not the only people on social media. Your employees and their families are there as well. This provides you with another avenue to talk and share with your employees.

Internal communications in business is a cornerstone of success. The less information dissemination to the troops, the worse off you are. The problem is that your employees, and people in general, have a need for information to fill in their blanks. If you are not providing that information, employees will create information that fills the void, and most often incorrectly. If a team of lawyers descend on your business to negotiate an employee stock offering and you are not sharing that information, you are likely to hear rumors that the company has been sold, or is under investigation, or who knows what.

Using Facebook or Twitter, for example, can let you spread little snippets of news to satisfy the questions on the minds of your employees and it doesn't require an hour of lost wages to get everyone in the conference room for a discussion.

Those platforms are also good for emergency management. If there is an active shooter in your office complex, or an ice storm, or earthquake, perhaps a tweet or a Facebook post can inform most everyone in your organization immediately, without having to resort to the slow and cumbersome nature of a call tree.

Restrict Access/Set Rules

It may seem odd that I have spent the last couple of pages touting the benefits of social media and now I am going to tell you to not let your employees use it. This isn't an absolute no-social-media rule, but some things need to be considered.

Internet use, in general, is a huge time suck, and social media makes it worse. Employees can easily get sucked down the rabbit hole and not stop until they find the end of the internet. And all because a friend posted a cat video to Facebook. As a business owner, you need to set policies that govern the use of social media. For example, (except for those employees using social media to perform their assigned duties) no social media in the workplace except during lunch, or after 5pm, or whatever time is appropriate for your organization. You can enforce this policy with technical controls such as a content filter (discussed later in the Cyber-Security chapter).

You also need to set forth a written policy for your employees that indicates what types of information about the company, its employees, and its customers should and should not be posted on social media. I would advise you to talk to your legal counsel about any social media policy you create, as the National Labor Relations Board has a lot to say about what you can and can't do about it.

BYOD or COPE

Thinking about yourself and your employees, who do you know that doesn't have a smart phone or tablet? I mean, other than cranky old Charlie who is still using that IBM Selectric and listening to Sha Na Na over there in his cubicle? Most everybody, probably, and certainly everyone under 40.

With this proliferation of mobile devices, employees are constantly wanting to use their personal phone, tablet, or other devices to access corporate email or files. Their motivation is usually pure. They want to get their job done. Unfortunately, as seemingly innocent as this action is, it is fraught with pitfalls, from data leakage to full-scale system compromises.

Regardless of the risk, the evolution of personal mobile devices and the rise of how necessary they are to business success these days are forcing many small business owners to make a choice. BYOD or COPE? Or, "Bring Your Own Device" vs. "Corporate Owned, Personally Enabled". They both have pluses and minuses, and need a little more explanation.

BYOD

BYOD is simply allowing your employees to access email and other business data on their personal devices, or to use their personal devices in the execution of your business. According to the CDW 2012 Small Business Mobility Report, 89% of small-business employees use their personal mobile devices for work. But the headache involved here is how do you support and secure all of these devices? The scary thing is that most small businesses don't even try! The CDW survey found that only 1 in 5 small businesses have deployed (or plan to deploy) any system for managing and securing employees' personal devices.

Allowing your corporate data, customer data, intellectual property, financial records and more to exist on unsecured, unmanaged mobile devices, specifically ones that you don't own, could put your organization at considerable risk, unless you take a proactive management role.

COPE

Is COPE any better? A minority of small businesses have implemented a Corporate Owned, Personally Enabled policy instead. They buy their employees' mobile devices, secure them, and then let employees load additional personal applications that they want or need. And the employers control what types of apps can be added, too. And the "personally enabled" aspect of COPE allows employees to choose the company-approved device they prefer while permitting them to use it both personally and professionally. COPE is certainly more controlled and secure, but for a business with a limited budget, buying devices for every employee can add up pretty quickly. If you go the COPE route and are large enough to buy in volume, you can likely negotiate substantial discounts.

There are still concerns with COPE. For example, if you have client information that must be kept secure or other industry specific regulations regarding the security of client data, then COPE is likely your best approach. It takes out any gray area of whose data is whose. Plus, there is a certain comfort level in being able to recover or confiscate any device for any reason at any time to protect your company without any worries of device ownership.

The Trade-Off

Despite the numerous advantages of COPE, most small businesses will still choose BYOD because it can save them money. Here are two of Lawrence Reusing's (GM of Mobile Security at Imation) important rules for BYOD. Consider these when creating your mobile device policy (also see the section on Mobile Device Management in the Cyber-Security chapter).

- Assume employees will use personal devices on the corporate network even if they are told not to. 50% of employees use personal devices to take confidential data out of companies every day.

- Assume employees value convenience more than security. If your policies are inconvenient, employees will work around them.

Even if you buck the tide and decide that you do not want your employees using their own devices, you must create and enforce a BYOD or COPE policy. Otherwise, you have placed your business at great risk.

Managing a COPE implementation is expensive and difficult. You have a constant flood of "Can I upgrade?", "I dropped my phone in the toilet.", and "I would rather have an iPhone." I would recommend going with a BYOD policy. It is easier, and cheaper, and resistance is futile. Provide your employees with a locate, lock, wipe, and anti-virus service to go with it, and insist on it as a condition for use, and you are golden. (And yes, phones need anti-virus too.)

File Share and Sync

In business, data is king. Businesses are creating documents, presentations, videos, and spreadsheets at a prolific pace. Generally, these documents reside in one of two places. One location is on the file server at the office, where people in the office have access to it. Due to the increasing mobility of business and the emergence of BYOD, the other location is on an employee's laptop, tablet, or other mobile device, because they often work outside the office and need access to those documents. This creates a couple of distinct problems.

Problem #1 is that the document created on the portable device is not readily available to the rest of the organization. Problem #2 is that if it is available to the rest of the organization, it is often in the form of a copy. Therefore, when the document gets updated at the office, those changes are not reflected in the copy on the mobile device and vice versa. So now which document is the correct one? What changed since the last one? This is particularly important with a contract, a sales order, or similar documents.

One of the hottest technologies now is that of file share and sync. If you have heard of Google Drive or Drop Box, then you have an idea of what I am talking about. If not, let me explain.

With file share and sync technology, a small application is installed on each device (desktop, laptop, phone, tablet, Mac, PC...) that allows users to share data, in a protected fashion, from anywhere there is an internet connection. So when the contract is updated in the office, it is the same contract presented to the customer on the other side of the nation. With the salesperson at the customer site, the customer requests a change and that change is immediately reflected in the fulfillment document at the office.

Using file share and sync, employees can work from home, a hotel room, the beach, or the lake, with secure access to a full suite of your corporate data, and be assured that it is the latest and greatest.

As Google Drive and Drop Box are consumer-grade products, they do not have appropriate features, controls, or security for handling business data, but there are many solutions out there that do; too many to mention here. So make sure when you are considering a file share and sync solution, you are using an enterprise-grade product.

Enterprise file share and sync (EFSS) solutions seamlessly integrate with your operating system, looking just like another folder or group of folders on your device. When a document is written to that folder, or updated in that folder, an identical folder on all other linked devices is automatically updated with the changes. An EFSS should either support file-locking which ensures that no file is being edited by two people at once, or provide the ability to have simultaneous editors.

The documents stored in an EFSS are continually backed up, and backup copies can be held for a pre-determined retention period. If a document is incorrectly modified, an EFSS will allow you to revert back to a previous version, or versions of the same file. This lets you roll back to a version that was saved just before it was infected by a virus, or edited by that idiot Steve, again. Sigh…

Most EFSS products are compliant with high security standards and provide encryption protocols for the data. Make sure, though, that when you are selecting a file sync and share solution that it is compliant with the regulations that cover your business, such as HIPAA, PCI, or Sarbanes-Oxley.

Consider EFSS for your mobile workforce, or your entire workforce. The convenience is unparalleled and it is cheaper than buying and maintaining your own file servers.

Internet Telephony (VoIP)

Internet telephony, also known as VoIP (Voice over Internet Protocol, or Voice over IP) is one of the more transformative technologies to come along in a while. In a nutshell, VoIP (pronounced "voyp") is using the internet to make phone calls, but it is so much more than that.

Imagine sending and receiving business calls from the golf course, or the airport, or your kitchen table, and it looks to the world like you are still at the office. Or what about voice mail messages being delivered to your e-mail inbox? But here is the big one – imagine doing those things and much more, and still dramatically reducing your phone bill.

Before I go much further, let me apologize. I don't know of any other technology on the internet that has more acronyms than VoIP, but it is essential you know some of these, so that when you are talking to your provider, you have some clue as to what the heck they are talking about. Please bear with me, and I will try to keep it to a minimum.

How does VoIP Work?

Before going into how VoIP works, an overview of telephony in general is necessary. So let's start with our second big acronym, POTS, or Plain Old Telephone Service. (Seriously, that's really what it stands for.) Back in the day, for telephone service you needed a pair of copper wires that ran from your phone to the PSTN (Public Switched Telephone Network, acronym #3). Somewhere, someone picks up their own phone, dials 867-5309, some relays click in the CO (Central Office, #4), your pair of wires gets connected to their pair of wires and the two of you are chatting away, just like Mr. Bell intended. Oh, and Uncle Sam gets to charge you fees and taxes on those wires to help subsidize rural, high-cost telephone exchanges. That worked well for a long time, and is still very much in use today, but business needed more.

Businesses generally need phone systems, not just phone lines, as there is need to transfer calls, conference call, and have higher call density (more folks on the phone at the same time). In a case like this, dragging in dozens of copper wire pairs is expensive, and generally featureless. So, many businesses will install a PBX (Primary Branch eXchange, #5), also known as a phone system. While you can connect your PBX to the PSTN using a POTS line… Hold up, let's try that again. While you can connect your phone system to the telephone company using plain old phone lines, a more common way to do it is by using a PRI (Primary Rate Interface, #6).

A PRI is a dedicated data line that allows up to 23 simultaneously active phone calls between your phone system and the rest of the world. You can sometimes buy a half, or even a quarter PRI, though they are still expensive and beholden to the tax man. But for this substantial cost you get excellent, guaranteed call quality. Understand that you can have huge numbers of physical phones and assigned phone numbers as part of a PBX using PRI, but unless you bring in more PRIs, you can't get more than 23 simultaneous calls.

In comes SIP (Session Initiating Protocol, #7). SIP is a method of connecting your phone system to the public telephone network using your broadband connection. This allows you to use some portion of your existing internet connection to make phone calls. The faster your internet connection, the more simultaneous calls you can potentially make, depending on how your system is configured. Now that you have connected your phone system to your phone carrier using SIP, you just escaped paying the tax man the antiquated excise and subsidy taxes that are applied to regular phone lines. You likely will get unlimited long-distance as part of the deal as well. While SIP can dramatically reduce your phone bills, there is a catch.

PRI has a guaranteed voice quality, meaning the phone company will promise that you won't get static, noise, or interruptions. SIP, however, is considered a best effort technology, meaning everyone will try to do their best, but no promises. Traditional phone calls using POTS or PRI are considered to be circuit-switched, meaning a dedicated circuit (think two copper wires) connects each end of the call, and in so, quality can be managed. SIP is different, and uses a packet-switched technology, which bears some explanation.

Imagine that your voice is a completed jigsaw puzzle, and you are talking to your mom on the other side of town. When you speak, the jigsaw puzzle (your voice) is broken apart, and each piece (aka packet) is sent by individual taxi to your mom's house. The cabs all get to choose their own route, and arrive at your mom's in a random order. The cabbies meet in your mom's driveway and give their best effort to putting the puzzle back together, even if one of the cabbies was mugged on the way, and another is hopelessly lost. Your mom gets a puzzle that is sometimes incomplete, but still very identifiable. That is the essence of packet-switching.

In the early days of VoIP, a reputation was gained about very poor call quality, and that reputation has unfortunately stuck. The reality, however, is that due to better management techniques and technical improvements, nowadays call quality is significantly better, and often VoIP calls are indistinguishable from regular circuit switched calls. If you regularly conduct business on your mobile phone, regardless of which carrier you have, then the voice quality of VoIP should be more than sufficient for you, as VoIP will typically exceed the quality of a cellular call by a good measure. If, however, voice quality is primary consideration for you, you may not want to consider the switch just yet. If you are on the fence about VoIP, ask your vendor to let you test a VoIP phone for a while, and you should be able to get your answer that way.

The Benefits of VoIP

There are many reasons to choose VoIP instead of the more traditional PRI and POTS solutions. Primary of these is operational costs, which are greatly reduced; but the benefits go even further:

- With VoIP, businesses do not need to maintain separate networks for phone and data, and moving a phone line to a new office is as simple as carrying the VoIP phone in there and plugging it in. No more expensive service calls to punch down copper wires.
- Depending on your phone system configuration, you can take your phone anywhere there is a broadband internet connection, plug in and start taking calls.
- You can get voice mail and faxes delivered to your e-mail inbox, and send them as well; a technique referred to as Unified Messaging.
- You can create local phone numbers in another city or state, without actually being there, making it easier for your customers to feel you are a "local" business.

- You can have your phone system ring your desk, your mobile, and your home phone all at the same time so you never miss a call. Productivity will be positively impacted by not playing games like "phone tag".

This list is just a sample, as the benefits of VoIP are ever-increasing. Every day, vendors are releasing more and more compelling features, which are driving businesses to VoIP in droves.

The Drawbacks of VoIP

Nothing is perfect, and VoIP is not an exception. There are a few issues with VoIP that are worth considering.

One major problem with VoIP is also its major strength. The strength is that your calls travel the internet just like data, which saves you money. The weakness is that when there is no power, there is no internet and there is no phone. Some VoIP systems will allow you to ring an alternate number, such as your mobile phone, in the event of a power outage, which reduces this issue to a large degree.

Another issue is with Emergency 911. With a traditional telephony solution, your location can be tracked automatically. Unfortunately, due to the work-from-anywhere nature of VoIP, that tracking is not automatic. The system must be kept updated as to where the phone is actually located. Some companies will opt to install a POTS line dedicated to 911, but that only works well when all phones are inside the location where the POTS lines are located.

Additionally, Fax machines are generally not VoIP enabled, and I really haven't noticed a push by the vendors to get them there. While they are still a fixture in most offices, Fax machines are being used less and less (being killed off by PDF and e-mail). Offices that want to keep their Fax machines up and running may choose to use one of the converters that are available now, or perhaps share the Emergency 911 POTS line with the Fax machine.

Hybrid Environments

Generally speaking, POTS, PRI, and SIP were used to describe how to connect your local phone system to the internet. There are situations where a combination of these technologies might be appropriate.

Imagine your business is a call center. Phone calls are what pays the bills, and what creates a lot of them too. You really want the cost savings associated with VoIP/SIP, but if the power goes out there in Squirrel Branch, Kentucky, you still have to be able to make calls. In a situation like this, you may want to install both PRI and SIP, using SIP to get the benefit of the unlimited long distance, and having the PRI available only in a fail-over situation. You won't save as much money, but you will always be able to generate revenue on your calls, whether or not a squirrel got into a transformer down the street.

Another hybrid situation is one where call quality is essential, but the flexibility of VoIP is equally important. Let's say you are a law firm who spends hours each day on the phone with high-dollar clients. In a case like this, you may want your internal phone system, or PBX, to be VoIP, giving you all the promised flexibility, yet be connected to your phone carrier over PRI, making sure the call quality from the phone system to carrier is of high quality. Inside your network, your IT provider can make quality adjustments to your local network which can greatly enhance call quality internally, as well, ensuring that your connection from your handset to your PBX is high-quality. The PRI will ensure the connection from your PBX to your telephone carrier is also high-quality. As long as the person on the other end has similar or better call quality, everything will be fine.

The Real Deal

There is such a movement towards VoIP, such a proliferation of mobile devices, and such an entrenched number of POTS and PRI circuits, you never know which technology the person on the other end might be using. POTS and PRI, with their greater expense and promise of call quality sound just like a cell phone call when you are talking to someone on a cell phone. Call quality defaults to the lowest common denominator. With a large segment of the population using mobile phones and VoIP, it really doesn't make sense to pay for call quality that you are only going to get sometimes, especially when that will happen less and less as economics becomes the driver for VoIP.

I would advocate that your business explore VoIP if for nothing else but reduced costs. You will likely be surprised how much more efficient you can make your business along the way by leveraging the technology to its extreme.

5 Cyber-Security Essentials

"Hackers are breaking the systems for profit. Before, it was about intellectual curiosity and pursuit of knowledge and thrill, and now hacking is big business". - Kevin Mitnick

Generally, there are two types of small businesses when it comes to cyber-security: victims, and potential victims. Simply put, most small businesses do not have adequate defensive measures in place to protect them from the ever-expanding cyber-threat. This is due to a number of reasons, but it often boils down to business owners not having a full understanding of the extent or seriousness of threats, not believing they are at risk, or having become desensitized to the warnings.

Consider this:

- Smaller businesses have become bigger targets for cyber-criminals because the bad guys know that they have fewer defense resources than large enterprises. (Source: National Cyber Security Alliance, StaySafeOnline.org)

- Half of all cyber-attacks are aimed at small- to medium-sized businesses. (Source: Forbes Article, "5 Ways Small Businesses Can Protect Against Cybercrime")

While these facts should be enough to convince business owners to focus more on their security, there is a larger problem, that of believing they have adequate security because they are running an anti-virus program, or they have a firewall.

Admittedly, firewalls and anti-virus programs are good first steps, and are foundational to any IT security posture, but they fall way short of adequate. Any good security strategy uses a layered security model, called defense-in-depth. Think of these layers as randomly stacked Swiss cheese slices. If you lay the firewall slice down, you see some holes, and what you see through the holes is your exposure to cyber-attack, called the attack surface. Now, when you add the anti-virus slice to the stack, some of the holes are covered or reduced in size, thereby reducing your vulnerability to attack. By continuing to stack layers, such as anti-malware, content-filtering, heuristic scanning, and intrusion detection, you continue to reduce your exposure to all manner of cyber-risk. (If you are wondering whether there is a slice of American cheese that will cover all of the holes, there is. Simply turn your computer off and leave it that way.)

Certainly, the defense-in-depth strategy sounds expensive, and perhaps by some measure it is. But if you consider the cost of a data breach or malware remediation, it will seem cheap in comparison. The good news is that there are new products on the market, such as Unified Threat Management (UTM) security appliances, that have most, if not all, of these slices already stacked for you, and at a greatly reduced cost over buying all of the individual technologies and implementing them singularly.

It is an unfortunate place where we are in terms of the internet and cyber-crime. The internet has likely done more for the improvement of the human condition than anything since electricity. It has also created, and continues to create, millions of invisible criminals, just trying to find a way to steal your data and disrupt your business. Cyber-security is a battle, and it is not one that you can win. You can only fight it, or lose it. I would encourage all small business owners to take a serious look at the cyber-risk to their organization and take action to defend the thing that they have worked so hard to build.

The rest of this chapter will focus on all of those Swiss cheese slices that make for defense-in-depth. It is not essential to implement all of the items identified here, but understand that more is generally better. You need to evaluate your real exposure, and your tolerance for risk and choose wisely.

Firewall

A firewall is designed like the gate of a castle. Everything that comes into or out of the castle passes through that gate, and is inspected by the guards. The challenge here is to make sure the guards are paying attention to the right things.

With firewalls, there are two separate classes: consumer-grade and business-grade (with multiple sub-categories of business-grade). While both are firewalls, the guards at the business-grade firewall are more like the Royal Guard as opposed to their rent-a-cop counterparts in the consumer-grade devices.

A consumer-grade firewall, available at your local mass-market retailer, is designed to stop everything from coming in at the same time, letting everything go back out. This lets you surf the internet (outbound) without getting hacked by criminals (inbound). These firewalls don't care about content, they care about rules, and the rules state that you can go anywhere outside from inside. The problem here is that if you get a Trojan or other malware through email (something the firewall allowed you to go get), then that malware can start shipping your financial information off to the internet, because the rules say that anything headed from inside to outside is OK.

In a business-grade firewall, traffic in both directions is closely monitored and reported by the Royal Guard. They look for people trying to break in. They search bags and briefcases on the way in and out. And they are regularly trained to look for new threats to the kingdom. In the malicious email scenario above, the traffic would likely be stopped inbound, but if that failed, your financial information headed for the underworld would be stopped on the way out of the gate.

Despite their expense, I consider business-grade firewalls essential to a good security posture.

There is another variant of the business-grade firewall, as mentioned before, call the Unified Threat Management (UTM) appliance which, at its heart, is a firewall. However, a good UTM will also include, in a single hardware device, many of the features identified in the rest of this chapter, such as content filtering, intrusion detection and SPAM filtering. This bundled approach makes it much more affordable than buying each of the security features individually.

Anti-Malware/Anti-Virus

If you wonder what the difference is between malware (malicious software) and a computer virus, then you've come to the right place. All chickens are birds but not all birds are chickens, and all viruses are malware but not all malware are viruses.

The problem with this distinction, though, is that the anti-virus program you have installed on your computer looks for and blocks many types (but not all types) of malware. Truthfully, a true computer virus, according to the agreed upon definition, really is not seen much anymore. Now you typically see Trojans, spyware and worms, but not true viruses. For your part, however, simply calling everything a virus is a workable solution.

An anti-virus program is essential on any computing device, and I do mean any. Yes, that includes your Mac or your Linux machine. Gone are the days where a Mac is a safe haven. New exploits are released all the time, for all platforms.

I also recommend a paid version of any anti-virus program you choose to run. The reason is three fold. First, most free anti-virus programs are licensed "for personal use only", which puts your business at risk of getting sued for software piracy. Second, if a software product is free, then your personal information (used in signing up for the product) is likely what is for sale. Third, those free products have limited feature sets. They have included just enough functionality to make you feel good, while they market the higher quality product to you on a continual basis; *"We have detected a virus in filexyz.doc! Upgrade to the full version for $19.99 to remediate this issue."*

Malware programs are like anti-virus programs in that they look for Trojans, spyware, and worms, but they extend their search out further to even more insidious programs. Typically, malware programs scan for and remediate problems after they have been installed, while anti-virus programs focus on trying to stop the infection to start with.

My recommendation is to run both of these products, where appropriate. Not all products are perfect, and the combination of these two programs make the holes in the Swiss cheese a little bit smaller.

E-mail Protection

We all know how annoying SPAM can be. If not dealt with, you can find yourself sorting through a dozen SPAM emails to get to one legitimate message. These SPAM messages can also include all sorts of malware and phishing links, where they try to trick the user into doing something that can cause damage to the systems or data.

Ending SPAM is virtually impossible without simply turning off your e-mail completely, but there are steps that can be taken that will greatly reduce it. Whether your e-mail sever is in your office or hosted elsewhere, e-mail filters can greatly reduce the SPAM and phishing messages that get through. However, you must understand that the stricter you set your SPAM controls, the more likely that legitimate e-mail will get blocked as well, so it is a continual balancing act.

There are bigger, faster, better, stronger alternatives coming out all the time to address this issue, so it is worth constantly looking at other options. However, better and more complex go hand-in-hand, and more complex often leads to misconfigured. Train your users (or have someone else train them) in the essential security measures regarding e-mail use, and never ever allow employees to use business e-mail for personal use and vice versa. You don't want the user's business e-mail address making it to a SPAM list somewhere.

Content Filtering

"It was the best of times. It was the worst of times." This is the Tale of Two Internets.

The sheer volume of information on the internet has enhanced the human condition. There are documents, processes, techniques, how-to videos, and more. It is fantastic business tool. It has connected families and friends across the globe. It is a fantastic social tool. It has pornography, gambling, violence, and fanaticism that simply doesn't belong in the workplace unless you are a terrorist sect.

The business internet is essential to many businesses, and can be used as a tool to grow your business. But along with this, comes social media and ecommerce. These activities can be a huge time suck, costing businesses a lot of money on lost productivity, as employees are catching up with family and shopping for the perfect pair of pumps while on the clock.

Then there is the dark side of the internet, with girls, guns, and gangstas. While they can also be a time suck, the larger issue here is the exposing your business to legal risk. If you have an employee that is visiting violence-promoting websites all day and winds up shooting up the office, you have a legal problem. If you don't take steps to intervene in the activities of the porn-watching sales guy, the sexual harassment claim by your office manager is going to have some teeth when it gets to the courtroom.

This is all easily mitigated with content filtering. A content filter can be part of a business-grade firewall, part of a stand-alone content appliance, or even part of your anti-virus solution.

These products work by categorizing websites into related groups such as Shopping, Business, Gambling and so on. You simply tell the content filter that you want to allow those websites classified as Business sites all of the time, Social Media at lunchtime only, and Violence and Pornography never. Now when Leon wants to leer at some hot chicks in his cubicle, he is met with a blocked screen and you get an email letting you know what Leering Leon is up to.

By the way, when you first implement a content filter, you will learn a lot about your employees that might just shock you. Timid Tina is into semi-automatic weapons in a serious, troubling way.

Another benefit of content filtering is that they tend to know about malicious, virus-laden websites and block them before a virus infection can happen. Understand that you don't have to click on anything to get a virus from these sites. All you have to do is visit it.

I consider content filtering every bit as essential as a firewall and anti-virus software. Certainly, it has the ability to protect you against many types of malware, but it also helps protect against the hostile workplace claims as well.

Training

If cyber-security can be thought of as a chain, then people are the weakest link. It is not (usually) intentional behavior that causes problems. In my experience, most security events are caused by dumb behavior... sorry, uneducated behavior.

I don't want to make you feel bad, since you have read this far, so I am going to use one of your employees as an example instead. Let's consider Chris who works in the sales department. Chris gets out of his car at the office one morning and sees a CD on the ground marked "2015 Salary & Bonus Data". Chris races to his desk and pops the CD in to see if that jerk Ed is making more than him. Then it is over. In the second it took to open the disk, the auto-run program dropped some malicious code into the machine, the machine phones home to the dark internet, and someone in Hackerstan has remote control over your network. In just seconds. Or less.

Let's say someone in accounting gets an email from *the.boss@yourcompnay.com*. It has all the appearances of coming from you, except your email is *the.boss@yourcompany.com*. The email directs the employee to transfer $25,631 to a specific account, immediately. Since it came from the boss (apparently), the employee does just what was asked, without any follow up. Now you are out 25 grand. You can't un-ring that bell, and this happens all of the time. This is not some fantastical made-up story. I have seen the emails in our own inboxes and have knowledge of actual victims of this scam.

Software and appliances can't fix either of these scenarios. This must be fixed through continuing education and training. I recommend finding some coursework that can be administered to new-hires as well as annually for everyone. Just search the web for "cyber-security training online" and you should be able to find something appropriate to your organization.

Data Encryption

Data encryption is exactly what it sounds like; your data scrambled so no one but you can read it. It is an extra step in protecting your data that is helpful to your security stance.

Data encryption can be broken down as "at rest" and "in motion". Data encryption in motion is the act of encrypting data as it is transmitted over the internet, like an email message. Data-in-motion encryption is especially useful for transmitting privacy data, such as social security number and patient information. Many industries, like Title Attorneys and Mortgage Lenders, are required to use data-in-motion encryption when exchanging client information, but it is a good idea for any business that is transmitting personal data over the internet in any fashion.

Data-at-rest encryption is encryption of data where it is stored, like on your hard drive, or on your backup device. Data-at-rest encryption can further be broken down as disk-based or file-based.

With disk-based encryption, often included (but not enabled) as part of the operating system of your computer, you simply turn on encryption and the whole disk is automatically encrypted. This is easily implemented, but has a drawback. When you copy that file to a thumb drive, or include it in an email, the encryption is automatically removed, as it is no longer located on the disk that was encrypted.

With file-based encryption, you choose what files to encrypt on a file-by-file basis. This overcomes the decryption issues seen with disk-based encryption, but has its own drawbacks. As the number of encrypted files grow, file-based encryption becomes more difficult to manage.

All encryption suffers from one significant drawback: if you lose the key, you lose the data. Period. So when you do a full-disk encryption on your laptop, and forget the password, just go ahead and wipe the laptop hard drive clean, and start over. (Depending on the safeguards built into the product you are using, you might be able to save it, but the goal of the encryption is if you don't have the key, you don't get the jewels. The odds are against you.)

Data-at-rest encryption is well suited for mobile devices, such as a laptop or iPad with patient data on it, for example. If the device is lost or stolen, the data is considered safe. As evidence, the Health Information Portability & Accountability Act (HIPAA) that governs the handling of patient information, waives the requirement to notify patients of potentially lost data if the device and the data was encrypted. Encryption is the only safe harbor under the HIPAA law.

Think about how important the data is on your phone, laptop, and tablet, and encrypt accordingly.

Network Separation

Network separation is a critical component of a good security posture. Network separation simply creates multiple isolated zones in your network that may share a common firewall, but do not interact with each other.

In smaller businesses, it is a good approach to have guest access (your customers) on a separate network, while the business operates on one or more protected networks. Do you think Starbucks is giving every Tom, Dick, and Caffeine Addict access to their corporate network? Nope. They offer a guest network for just this purpose, and so should you.

Larger companies will go as far as separating departmental networks as well, due to the greater risk of insider threat. This approach may be unnecessary in smaller organizations, but as your business grows, ask yourself if the guys in sales really need access to company payroll records.

Modern networks (both wired and wireless) are not difficult (for a network engineer) to segment appropriately, and provide added security against the spread of malicious software and behaviors. Just something to consider as your business grows.

Intrusion Detection

Intrusion detection systems come in two flavors. Network Intrusion Detection Systems (or NIDS) which are designed to monitor networks and Host Intrusion Detection Systems (or HIDS) which are designed to monitor computers or hosts. Both look for out-of-the-ordinary network traffic that might indicate an intrusion is underway.

The NIDS is a network device that all network traffic passes through, like a TSA checkpoint. Everyone gets x-rayed before being allowed to pass. If the examiner notices something out of the ordinary, the wand-operator is notified to take additional actions. In the case of NIDS, the wand-operator is the systems administrator. NIDS systems are not as common on small business networks, but are here for completeness, as you will find them embedded in some business-class firewalls.

What you will find quite often in small business networks is a HIDS. A HIDS is a software product installed on your machine, usually as part of a larger anti-virus product. A HIDS typically knows what your system files look like in size, shape, and date, and monitors them for changes that might indicate an intrusion. If it detects a change, it will notify an administrator for resolution, or may be configured to take corrective action automatically.

While these products are not absolutely necessary, if they are available as part of your anti-virus product suite (which they would not be in freeware), or as part of your firewall, turn them on and use them. It is one more piece of Swiss cheese on the security sandwich.

Mobile Device Management

A mobile device is simply a computing device that can be operated without a power cord or network cable. Think laptops, tablets, phones, or any other portable device that contains your business applications or data.

Mobile devices are fantastic for productivity, as they allow your employees to work from anywhere, but due to their portability, they are also at risk of being lost, as is the data on them, putting your business information in the wind.

Imagine your HR person puts a list of employee names, addresses, and social security numbers on her laptop to take home and work on for the weekend. She stops by the Quick-Rip Gas & Grub on the way home. While she is in the store to pick up bottle of Boone's Farm Strawberry Hill, the laptop is stolen off the front seat of her Fiesta. Now, not only are you out a laptop, but you have to notify all of your employees that their identity is at risk, and maybe even need to buy them an Identity Protection policy. Not a good situation. Now what if it was your customer's data, or your patient's healthcare records?

There are Mobile Device Management (MDM) tools that make this much less of an issue. Whether it be a company-provided device or the user's personal device, these can be outfitted with software that allows you to do things like track the location of the devices, enable the camera to see who is using it, encrypt the data, lock the device, wipe the data off of the device, and more.

When your MDM-protected device is stolen, your chances of recovery are somewhat better, and you do have the ability to remotely remove the data from it to prevent unauthorized use.

Now you don't need to tell the best customer of your law firm that you have lost their intellectual property documents.

Generally, for just a few dollars a month per device, you can greatly reduce your risk of data loss. I would recommend you consider the risk of data loss/leakage to your organization, and evaluate the benefits that MDM might provide you.

Least Privilege

There is a security concept called Least Privilege. Least Privilege is the idea of only allowing a user access to those systems or data that is necessary in the performance of their duties. As an example, the receptionist is not allowed access to the accounting data or systems, and the accounting staff is not allowed access to data and systems in the Support department.

There are two reasons for this segmentation. First, if the receptionist falls victim to a phishing scam (a common target), the compromise of that user does not easily spread throughout the organization, particularly into the accounting systems.

The second reason for this segregation is to reduce the risk and exposure to insider threat. When Angry Arthur gets his performance review and finds he is ranked at the bottom of the heap and isn't getting a raise, his ability to destroy internal systems is limited. And know this, the threat of insider attack is very real, and the most difficult to defend against.

I will say that, taken to the extreme, Least Privilege can be difficult to manage and detrimental to productivity. A right-sized implementation, generally based on roles and not people, is easier to implement and manage, and is less impactful to productivity.

Two-Factor Authentication

Two-Factor Authentication (2FA) is a more secure method of system login than the traditional username and password, and should be considered for sensitive systems, particularly those with exposure to the internet.

The usual username and password approach is a single-factor authentication scheme, and if an attacker-hacker figures out the username (a very simple task), using a number of readily available tools and computer horsepower, they can crack most passwords in short order. Game over. Thanks for playing.

In a two-factor model, access is granted based on something you know, and something you have. The something you know is your username and password (factor 1). The something you have may be a passcode device, a cell phone that can receive text messages, a passcode app on your phone, a fingerprint, a retina image, a voiceprint, and so on. Think James Bond and you get a sense of how far it might go.

In a typical scenario, and end-user may log into an application or server with a username and password. However, before access is fully granted, the user receives a text message on their authorized phone that includes a 6-digit random number. This number is valid for 300 seconds. The user must enter the number correctly, and within the allotted time, to be granted access. What they know is their username/password. What the have is the phone that is allowed to receive the passcode. This makes for far more secure systems.

2FA isn't appropriate for everything (yet) as it can sometimes be cumbersome to implement and manage. However, many companies are beginning to implement this technology. At the time of this writing, Amazon.com has recently announced their intention to implement 2FA, meaning it will become more familiar to the general user community. Consider the value of the data and systems you are protecting, and consider the added benefit of this measure. Perhaps 2FA is right for your organization.

Essential Security Policies

At a minimum, there are two security policies that you should have in place to help steer user behavior down a path that is consistent with good security. The minimum policy that every organization should have in place is an Acceptable Use Policy (AUP). If you are going to allow your employees to use personal devices to access your networks or data, in any fashion, you need a Bring Your Own Device (BYOD) policy as well.

Acceptable Use

An Acceptable Use Policy should explicitly define how the company technology resources should be used. It should also have clauses that explicitly state the enforcement criteria and disciplinary actions that can be taken, such as suspension or termination, in the case of flagrant violation.

Any AUP should contain language similar to the following sample clauses:

General Use and Ownership

- While Bob's Bagels' management desires to provide a reasonable level of privacy, users should be aware that the data they create, or any non-licensed or copyrighted data stored on the corporate information systems, remains the property of Bob's Bagels. Because of the need to protect Bob's Bagels' network and business interests, management cannot guarantee the confidentiality of information stored on any network device belonging to Bob's Bagels. This includes, but is not limited to, data files, email, voice mail, and other data types.

- Employees are responsible for exercising good judgment regarding the reasonableness of personal use. Employees should be guided by this policy, and if there is any uncertainty, employees should consult their supervisor or manager.
- For security and network maintenance purposes, as well as any other need necessitated by the best interest of Bob's Bagels, authorized individuals within Bob's Bagels may monitor equipment, systems and network traffic at any time, and without notice.
- Bob's Bagels reserves the right to audit networks and systems on a periodic basis to ensure compliance with this policy.

Security and Proprietary Information

- Confidential information includes, but is not limited to company private, corporate strategies, competitor sensitive, trade secrets, specifications, customer lists, and research data. Employees should take all necessary steps to prevent unauthorized access to this information.
- Keep passwords secure and do not share accounts. Authorized users are responsible for the security of their passwords and accounts. System-level passwords should be changed in accordance with domain policy and accepted standards.
- Because information contained on portable computers is especially vulnerable, special care should be exercised. Protect laptops from unauthorized access in accordance with common sense practices.
- Postings by employees from a Bob's Bagels' email address to newsgroups should contain a disclaimer stating that the opinions expressed are strictly their own

and not necessarily those of Bob's Bagels, unless posting is in the course of business duties.

- All hosts used by the employee that are connected to the Bob's Bagels Internet/Intranet/Extranet, whether owned by the employee or Bob's Bagels, shall be continually executing approved virus-scanning software with a current virus database updates, unless overridden by departmental or group policy.
- Employees must use extreme caution when opening e-mail attachments received from unknown senders, which may contain viruses, e-mail bombs, or Trojan horse code.

Unacceptable Use

The following activities are, in general, prohibited. Employees may be exempted from these restrictions during the course of their legitimate job responsibilities (e.g., systems administration staff may have a need to disable the network access of a host if that host is disrupting production services).

Under no circumstances is an employee of Bob's Bagels authorized to engage in any activity that is illegal under local, state, federal or international law while utilizing Bob's Bagels-owned resources.

System and Network Activities

The following activities are strictly prohibited, with no exceptions:

- Violations of the rights of any person or company protected by copyright, trade secret, patent or other intellectual property, or similar laws or regulations, including, but not limited to, the installation or distribution of "pirated" or other software products that are not appropriately licensed for use by Bob's Bagels.

- Unauthorized copying of copyrighted material including, but not limited to, digitization and distribution of photographs from magazines, books or other copyrighted sources, copyrighted music, and the installation of any copyrighted software for which Bob's Bagels or the end user does not have an active.

- Exporting software, technical information, encryption software or technology, in violation of international or regional export control laws, is illegal. The appropriate management should be consulted prior to export of any material that is in question.

- Introduction of malicious programs into the network or server (e.g., viruses, worms, Trojan horses, e-mail bombs, etc.).

- Revealing your account password to others or allowing use of your account by others. This includes family and other household members when work is being done at home.

- Using a Bob's Bagels computing asset to actively engage in procuring or transmitting material that is in violation of sexual harassment or hostile workplace laws in the user's local jurisdiction. Material in this category includes, but is not limited to, sexually suggestive or explicit documents, images, videos, and audio files.

- Using a Bob's Bagels computing asset to actively engage illegal activities, such as online gambling.

- Making fraudulent offers of products, items, or services originating from any Bob's Bagels account.

- Making statements about warranty, expressly or implied, unless it is a part of normal job duties.

- Effecting security breaches or disruptions of network communication. Security breaches include, but are not limited to, accessing data of which the employee is not an intended recipient, or logging into a server or account that the employee is not expressly authorized to access, unless these duties are within the scope of regular duties. For purposes of this section, "disruption" includes, but is not limited to, network sniffing, pinged floods, packet spoofing, denial of service, and forged routing information for malicious purposes.

- Port scanning or security scanning except by designated administrative personnel as part of assigned duties.
- Executing any form of network monitoring which will intercept data not intended for the employee's host, unless this activity is a part of the employee's normal job/duty.
- Circumventing user authentication or security of any host, network, or account.
- Interfering with or denying service to, any user other than the employee's host (for example, denial of service attack).
- Using any program/script/command, or sending messages of any kind, with the intent to interfere with, or disable, a user's terminal session, via any means, locally or via the Internet/Intranet/Extranet.
- Providing information about, or lists of, Bob's Bagels' employees to parties outside Bob's Bagels.

Email and Communications Activities

- Sending unsolicited email messages, including the sending of "junk mail" or other advertising material to individuals who did not specifically request such material (email SPAM).
- Any form of harassment via email, telephone or paging, whether through language, frequency, or size of messages.
- Unauthorized use, or forging, of email header information.
- Solicitation of email for any other email address, other than that of the poster's account, with the intent to harass or to collect replies.

- Creating or forwarding "chain letters", "Ponzi" or other "pyramid" schemes of any type.

These example clauses should be considered for any AUP, but can be amended to better fit your organization. Also, I would advise that every employee, at the time they hire in, and annually thereafter at the employee review, read and sign the AUP.

BYOD

If your organization allows BYOD (see earlier section on Bring Your Own Device), I would highly recommend implementing a BYOD policy. A good BYOD policy should spell out the activities and criteria for safe behavior for systems accessing company data, and should include clauses such as following:

- Devices must use the following operating systems: Android X.x or later, iOS X.x or higher.
- Devices must store all user-saved passwords in an encrypted password store.
- Devices must be configured with a secure password that complies with Bob's Bagels' password policy. This password must not be the same as any other credentials used within the organization.
- With the exception of those devices managed by Bob's Bagels, devices are not allowed to be connected directly to the internal corporate network.
- Users must report all lost or stolen devices used to access company data to Bob's Bagels IT immediately.
- If a user suspects unauthorized access to company data via a mobile device, they must report the incident to Bob's Bagels immediately.
- Devices must not be jailbroken or rooted or have any software/firmware installed designed to gain access to prohibited applications.

- Users must not load pirated software or illegal content onto their devices.
- Applications must only be installed from approved sources, such as Google Play or the Apple app store. Installation of apps from untrusted sources is forbidden.
- Devices must be kept up to date with manufacturer provided patches. As a minimum, patches should be checked weekly and applied at least once a month.
- Devices must not be connected to any (personal or corporate) PC without up-to-date and enabled anti-malware protection or which does not comply with corporate policy.
- Devices must be encrypted in line with Bob's Bagels' compliance standards.
- Users should not merge personal and work e-mail accounts on their devices. They must only send company data through the corporate e-mail system. If a user suspects that company data has been sent from a personal email account, either in body text or as an attachment, they must notify Bob's Bagels IT immediately.
- Users must not connect the mobile device to corporate workstations for any purpose, including synchronization and backup of media files, unless such content is required for legitimate business purposes.

As with the Acceptable Use Policy, this policy should also include disciplinary actions for violations, and have an initial and annual acceptance procedure.

Cyber Insurance

So after you have put in some, most, or all of those security precautions I just wrote about, you are feeling pretty good, aren't you? Well, not so fast. Nothing is perfect, and to protect yourself and your small business, I would recommend cyber insurance. Seriously, if you handle customer data, I would recommend that you take out a cyber insurance policy to protect yourself in case of a breach or data loss.

I know you still may not believe that you are a target, but hackers are looking for businesses of any size with valuable customer data they can steal and sell on the black market. It happens all the time, but it's just not reported, mostly because of the expected customer backlash.

Cyber insurance can include data loss, breach notifications, fines, legal representation, and so forth. It can even cover lost income due to systems outages, as well as third-party losses to your customers and vendors.

Talk to your insurance agent about the value and the price of a cyber insurance policy. Likely, for a few hundred dollars a year, you can protect yourself from unexpected losses. You probably have a better chance of getting hacked than your car getting stolen, and you have insurance on the car, right? Right?

6 Minimum Security Measures

"I think computer viruses should count as life. I think it says something about human nature that the only form of life we have created so far is purely destructive. We've created life in our own image." –
Stephen Hawking

If you just want to know what the least amount you can do and still have some measure of protection, I understand. Successful small businesses are often budget conscious, if nothing else. While I would advocate you take long-term look at your IT budgeting to make room for more robust security protections, the here and now, in terms of budgets vs. security, must be addressed.

I don't want to be an alarmist, but dangerous and well-funded cyber-crime rings in China, Russia, and the Ukraine, among other places, are using sophisticated software systems to hack into thousands of small businesses like yours to steal credit cards, client information, and swindle money directly out of your bank account. Some are even being funded by their own government to attack businesses, particularly those in the US.

What is even worse is that there are tens of thousands of "script kiddies" out there, the stereotypical teenage boy sitting at the computer in his parent's basement, downloading and running freely-available hacking scripts designed to steal your data. They don't even have to be smart to run the scripts, just motivated to make a couple of bucks.

Both of these groups are involved in an aggressive, continual, and escalating campaign for financial gain, and have little fear of being caught or prosecuted.

Don't think you're in danger because you're "small" and not a big fish like a Target or Home Depot? Think again. 82,000 new malware threats are being released every single day and half of the cyber-attacks occurring are aimed at small businesses; you just don't hear about it because it's kept quiet for fear of attracting bad PR, lawsuits, data-breach fines, and out of sheer embarrassment.

In fact, the National Cyber Security Alliance reports that one in five small businesses have been victims of cybercrime in the last year – and that number is growing rapidly as more businesses utilize cloud computing, mobile devices, and store more information online. You can't turn on the TV or read the news without learning about the latest online data breach, and government fines and regulatory agencies are growing in number and severity. Because of all of this, it's critical that you have at least a minimum set of security measures in place.

The remainder of this chapter identifies these essential protections you really should implement, and in short order.

Train Employees On Security Best Practices

The #1 vulnerability for business networks is the employees using them. It's extremely common for an employee to infect an entire network by opening and clicking a phishing e-mail (that's an e-mail cleverly designed to look like a legitimate e-mail from a website or vendor you trust). If they don't know how to spot infected e-mails or online scams, they could compromise your entire network. To learn more about phishing, Google "how to recognize phish attempts".

Create an Acceptable Use Policy (AUP)

An AUP outlines how employees are permitted to use company-owned PCs, devices, software, Internet access and e-mail. Put a policy in place that limits the web sites employees can access with work devices and Internet connectivity. Further, you have to enforce your policy with content-filtering software and firewalls. Best practices suggest setting up permissions and rules that will regulate what websites your employees access and what they do online during company hours and with company-owned devices. Best practices also support giving certain users more "freedom" than others, which tends to increase employee productivity.

Having this type of policy is particularly important if your employees are using their own personal devices to access company e-mail and data.

If that employee is checking unregulated, personal e-mail on their own laptop that infects that laptop, it can be a gateway for a hacker to enter YOUR network. If that employee leaves, are you allowed to erase company data from their phone? If their phone is lost or stolen, are you permitted to remotely wipe the device – which would delete all of that employee's photos, videos, texts, etc. – to ensure your clients' information isn't compromised?

Further, if the data in your organization is highly sensitive, such as patient records, credit card information, financial information and the like, you may not be legally permitted to allow employees to access it on devices that are not secured; but that doesn't mean an employee might not innocently "take work home". If it's a company-owned device, you need to detail what an employee can or cannot do with that device, including "rooting" or "jail-breaking" the device to circumvent security mechanisms you put in place.

Require Strong Passwords and Passcodes to Lock Mobile Devices

Passwords should be at least 8 characters and contain lowercase and uppercase letters, symbols, and at least one number. On a cell phone, requiring a passcode to be entered will go a long way toward preventing a stolen device from being compromised. Again, this can be enforced by your network administrator so employees don't get lazy and choose easy-to-guess passwords, putting your organization at risk. (Did you know that the 1000 most common passwords are used 75% of the time? And all of them can be guessed by cyber-criminals?)

Keep Your Network Up-To-Date

New vulnerabilities are frequently found in common software programs you are using, such as Microsoft Office; therefore, it's critical you patch and update your systems frequently. If you're under a managed IT plan, this can all be automated for you so you don't have to worry about missing an important update.

Have an Excellent Backup

This can foil the most aggressive (and new) ransom-ware attacks, where a hacker locks up your files and holds them ransom until you pay a fee. If your files are backed up, you don't have to pay a crook to get them back. A good backup will also protect you against accidental (or intentional) file deletion or overwriting, natural disasters, fire, water damage, hardware failures, and a host of other data-erasing disasters. Again, your backups should be automated and monitored; the worst time to test your backup is when you desperately need it to work!

Don't allow employees to download unauthorized software or files

One of the fastest ways cyber-criminals access networks is by duping unsuspecting users to willfully download malicious software by embedding it within downloadable files, games, or other "innocent-looking" apps. This can largely be prevented with a good firewall combined with employee training and good end-point management and monitoring software.

Implement a Robust End-Point Anti-Virus/Anti-Malware Product

Don't believe that all anti-virus products are the same, and that you can save a few bucks by running one of the free alternatives. Make sure your anti-virus program protects against known as well as unknown threats, and provides web surfing and download management and control. This protection should extend to when the device is not connected to the corporate network as well.

Don't Scrimp On a Good Firewall

A firewall acts as the frontline defense against hackers, blocking everything you haven't specifically allowed to enter (or leave) your computer network. Consumer-grade firewalls are not suitable to the task of protecting your corporate network. Also, all firewalls need monitoring and maintenance, just like all devices on your network. This too should be done by your IT provider as part of their regular, routine maintenance.

If Nothing Else, Take out a Cyber-Insurance Policy

If you choose to do nothing, at least consider taking out an insurance policy to protect your business when something does happen. However, be prepared to pay a higher premium if you are not going to take the essential steps to protect yourself.

Make sure you don't fall into the "this will never happen to me" camp, or the "I'll deal with it if and when it happens" frame of mind. That laissez-faire attitude could easily spell disaster for your small business. If you can't implement these protections on your own, get an IT service provider to do it for you, but by all means, do it.

7 IT Management Concepts

"The first rule of any technology used in a business is that automation applied to an efficient operation will magnify the efficiency. The second is that automation applied to an inefficient operation will magnify the inefficiency." - Bill Gates

IT management isn't fundamentally different than managing any other department. You have budgets to create and manage, and both human capital and infrastructure resources to acquire, utilize, manage, and retire. There are just a couple of additional concepts that I want to touch on here.

Refresh Planning

If you are like many small business owners and managers, you are very conscious of everything you spend, and likely put off every possible purchase until the last moment. You often put great effort into purchasing the least expensive solution that meets the minimum suitability to the current need. This helps to manage cash flow and gives the appearance of a healthy bottom line. Good common sense, really. However, in some cases, such as with IT infrastructure investment, it simply masks an underlying business risk, and deserves more consideration.

The computer refresh plan at many small businesses is reactionary and very simple, based on the concept of "if it ain't broke, don't fix it." And when it does break, you likely run down to the big box store and get the cheapest, flavor-of-the-day, beige econo-box. In the just-in-time parlance of the day, what could be wrong with this scenario? Specifically, this approach is one that embraces emergency as a call to action, and guarantees unpredictable IT costs. Implementing a refresh plan easily mitigates both of these issues.

A good technology refresh plan can help your small business in several areas. It can help stabilize the technology environment; optimize IT spending, making it predictable and easy to budget; help increase productivity; and minimize revenue loss due to IT failures. There are other intangible benefits as well, such as enhanced customer satisfaction and improved employee morale that are impactful, while not quantifiable. If you have ever had a business apologize to you because their systems were down, or slow at the time you called or visited, then you know what I am talking about.

A good refresh plan is essential, easy to implement, and, in its simplest form, consists of buying business-class servers and desktops, well outfitted and properly warrantied, and replacing them every 3-5 years. Since that is somewhat contrary to "if it ain't broke...", let's talk about the benefits of these tenets.

First, business-class machines are more expensive, but are they worth it? Simply put, you get what you pay for. Business-class machines use higher quality parts and are better engineered for longevity, serviceability, and support. They break less and are repaired easier. Less breakage, less downtime, less repair costs, less lost revenue. The loss-leader model from the box-stores costs less up front, but can quickly eat up any savings with a single repair bill. The same holds true for purchasing a warranty. It seems counter-intuitive to pay more for a business-class machine and then pay even more for a warranty. Well, the warranty gets you faster and better service in case of a failure, and usually costs about the same or less than a typical repair bill. More than that, if in the rare event you do have a failure, you can get same-day or next-day service that is simply not available from most retail outlets, reducing revenue loss associated with downtime.

Second, the common (yet flawed) philosophy when it comes to IT refresh plans, getting back to "if it ain't broke...", is that it is easier to wait until a machine breaks and then replace it cheaply, as it has the appearance of saving money. Unfortunately, that is rarely the case, but it is difficult to quantify. A machine ships from the factory with a finite set of resources. The operating systems and applications, however, have an ever-increasing demand for those resources (due to security releases, patches, and upgrades) causing worsening performance over time. Think of a train that gets a few cars added to it at every train station. This reduced performance increases the time necessary for an end-user to complete a task. This results in an increase in support calls, which are intrusive and cause more delays in completing the task. Also, older, more cheaply built machines, are more inclined to fail, further delaying task completion. All this time adds up.

Let's use a legal office as an example. Assume an older machine is causing a lawyer to have 15 minutes less billable time a week, due to slow performance or service calls. And also assume a bill rate of $250/hr. That is $3250 annually, or about the cost of 3 business-class laptops. Given this scenario, stretching your expected duty cycle from 3 years out to five years could actually cost you $6,500.

Using the same fictional legal office, let's assume that one of the lawyer's machines fails on Monday morning. It will take most of the day to acquire a suitable replacement if it is available locally, or several days if it is shipped in. The machine needs to be outfitted with the correct software and connections, and the user's data, if previously backed up, needs to be restored. If all of that takes 2 days to get completed, you have lost $4,000 in billable time. Now, what if that lawyer was due in court with something that was on that machine? Now, what if that was the main server instead of a single laptop and none of the lawyers in the firm can bill? Ouch!

In my experience, a good refresh plan is essential to good business health, and has the following terms:

Buy business-class laptops and desktops with a 3-year warranty, and plan to replace them at the end of the warranty period. Each year, budget to replace 1/3 of your laptops and desktops. If absolutely necessary, you might let that slip a year or two depending on budget constraints and serviceability, but no longer. In that extended period after warranty expiration, when they do fail, replace them as opposed to spending money to repair them.

Buy business-class servers with as much capacity as you can afford at the time. Get the longest warranty that is offered (usually 3-5 years), and plan to replace them as soon as the warranty expires.

This refresh plan takes a proactive approach that allows your technology infrastructure to remain current, and keeps unpredictable repair costs to a minimum. As planned replacements can be performed in a scheduled, non-emergency fashion, they are considerably less impactful, less stressful, and more affordable.

As a small business owner, it makes good sense to implement a technology refresh plan, based on the new adage of "if it ain't broke is really the best time to fix it." It will have tangible and intangible benefits, and have a positive impact in many parts of your business. Certainly, business is an ever-changing environment, so use this plan as a guide, not as gospel, and it will serve you well, long term.

Budgeting

Now that you are armed with a good refresh plan, let's work on creating the basis for a predictable IT budget. Pretty simple, really, so long as you have selected a fully managed IT service plan, and are not using break/fix (See the chapter on the IT Support Models).

Let's start off by taking the replacement value of all of the technology in your office, multiply that by 1.05% to account for rising prices and divide that amount by three years (your refresh cycle). Add in all of your recurring expenditures for network, software, cell phones, VoIP services, copier/printer service and everything IT related. Assuming you have a managed service plan, multiply the quoted plan amount by 1.2, as your environment will likely incur some out of scope work, to the tune of up to 20% of your Managed Service fee. That should do it.

((Tech Value*1.05) / 3 years)) + (Recurring Expenditures) + (Managed Service Fee * 1.2) = IT budget.

Drop that number in your budget spreadsheet and you are going to end up pretty close, dollar-wise. A number you can plan for and work towards.

If on the other hand, you have stayed in the world of break/fix, and you are praying nothing bad happens, the formula will differ from the above only slightly, replacing the Managed Service Fee with the variable X, and will work a little something like the one below.:

((Tech Value*1.05) / 3 years)) + (recurring expenditures) + (X^{prayer}) = IT budget.

You cannot solve for the IT budget in the break/fix equation because the power of prayer, while formidable, is no way to manage a budget. If, for no other reason, I would advocate managed services so that you can predict, with uncanny accuracy, what your IT costs will be.

I will make one last recommendation regarding managing (and reducing) your budget. Shop your phone and network service every year, about 90 days prior to contract renewal, and tell your vendor you are looking into other alternatives. You will likely find there is wiggle room there to reduce your costs. These providers are well aware that it costs less to keep you as a customer than it does to get new customers. They will horse trade.

8 Survivability

"If the automobile had followed the same development cycle as the computer, a Rolls-Royce would today cost $100, get a million miles per gallon, and explode once a year, killing everyone inside." – Robert F. Cringely

I know everyone reading this book (both of you) might not live in tornado alley like I do. But you might live in earthquake-prone California, or the hurricane-vulnerable east coast. Regardless of where you are, there is the threat of both natural and man-made disasters knocking your business down. Take a few significant steps to ensure that your business doesn't just survive, but continues to thrive in the event of a natural disaster.

Disaster Recovery Plan

If your data is important to your business and you cannot afford to have your operations halted for days – even weeks – due to data loss or corruption, you need to prepare. A disaster can happen at any time on any day and is likely to occur at the most inconvenient time. (Really, though, when is a convenient time for a disaster?) If you aren't already prepared, you run the risk of having the disaster coming before you have a plan in place to handle it.

A workable disaster recovery plan should include the following components, at a minimum.

- Have a written plan. As simple as it may sound, just thinking through in advance what needs to happen if your server has a meltdown or a natural disaster wipes out your office, will go a long way in getting it back fast. At a minimum, the plan should contain details on what disaster could happen and a step-by-step process of what to do, who should do it, and how. Also include contact information for various service providers and username and password information for various key websites and systems. Writing this plan will also allow you to think about what you need to budget for backup, maintenance, and disaster recovery. If you can't afford to have your network down for more than a few hours, then you need a plan that can get you back up and running within that time frame. You may want the ability to virtualize your server, allowing the office to run off of the virtualized server while the real server is repaired. If you can afford to be down for a couple of days, there are cheaper solutions. Once written, print out a copy and store it in a fireproof safe, an offsite copy (at your home), and a copy with your IT vendor.
- Hire a trusted professional to help you. Trying to recover your data after a disaster without professional help is business suicide; one misstep during the recovery process can result in forever losing your data or result in weeks of downtime. Make sure you work with someone who has experience in both setting up business contingency plans (so you have a good framework from which you can restore your network), and experience in

data recovery. Better yet, build a survivable system to begin with. (More on that later.)

- Have a communications plan. If something should happen where employees couldn't access your office, e-mail or use the phones, how should they communicate with you? Make sure your plan includes this information, including multiple communications methods. (See Communication Plan at the end of this chapter.)

- Automate your backups. If backing up your data depends on a human being doing something, it's flawed. The #1 cause of data loss is human error (people not swapping out tapes properly, someone not setting up the backup to run properly, etc.). Always automate your backups so they run like clockwork.

- Have an offsite backup of your data. Always, always, always maintain a recent copy of your data off site, on a different server, or on a storage device. Onsite backups are good, but they won't help you if they get stolen, flooded, burned or hacked along with your server.

- Have remote access and management of your network. Not only will this allow you and your staff to keep working if you can't go into your office, but you'll love the convenience it offers. Plus, your IT staff or an IT consultant should be able to access your network remotely in the event of an emergency or for routine maintenance. Make sure they can.

- Image your server. Having a copy of your data offsite is good, but keep in mind that all that information has to be restored someplace to be of any use. If you don't have all the software disks and licenses, it could take days to reinstate your applications (like Microsoft Office, your database, accounting software, etc.) even though your data may be readily available. Imaging your server is similar to making an exact replica; that replica can then be copied to another server saving an enormous amount of time and money in getting your network back. Best of all, you don't have to worry about losing your preferences, configurations or favorites. To find out more about this type of backup, ask your IT professional.

- Have network documentation. Network documentation is simply a blueprint of the software, data, systems and hardware you have in your company's network. Your IT vendor should put this together for you. This will make the job of restoring your network faster, easier, and cheaper. It also speeds up the process of everyday repairs on your network since the technicians don't have to spend time figuring out where things are located and how they are configured. And finally, should disaster strike, you have documentation for insurance claims of exactly what you lost. Again, have your IT professional document this and keep a printed copy with your disaster recovery plan.

- Maintain Your System. One of the most important ways to avoid disaster is by maintaining the security of your network. While fires, floods, theft and natural disasters are certainly a threat, you are much more likely to experience downtime and data loss due to a virus, worm or hacker attack. That's why it's critical to keep your network patched, secure and up-to-date. Additionally, monitor hardware for deterioration and software for corruption. This is another overlooked threat that can wipe you out. Make sure you replace or repair aging software or hardware to avoid this problem.

- Test, test, test! A study conducted in October 2007 by Forrester Research and the Disaster Recovery Journal found that 50 percent of companies test their disaster recovery plan just once a year, while 14 percent never test. If you are going to go through the trouble of setting up a plan, then at least hire an IT pro to run a test once a month to make sure your backups are working and your system is secure. After all, the worst time to test your parachute is after you've jumped out of the plane.

Backup and Disaster Recovery

As discussed in the Backup Technology chapter, a good disk-based backup is essential for survivability of your business, in case of a disaster. As mentioned previously, disk-based backup is far superior to tape backup, as it is faster and more dependable.

In my opinion, the new imaged-based Backup and Disaster Recovery (BDR) systems are essential technology to any business reliant on their data. They may be a little more expensive than more traditional backup systems, but definitely worth the money.

The BDR devices make a full working copy of your servers, often once or more per hour. If disaster strikes, you can literally boot a virtualized copy of the server and begin working on it in minutes.

Let me provide a disaster scenario as an explanation of the utility, and cost justification of such a device. Let's say that your company, Fred's Fire Trucks, refurbishes and sells used fire trucks around the globe. You have a staff of sales people whose primary tools are your in-house ERP system and a desk phone, and they spend all day selling fire trucks from Dubuque to Dubai. Let's also assume you are smart enough to have invested in a VoIP phone system for the benefits it brings to the table.

It was a dark and stormy night…

Hurricane Horatio is raging up the eastern seaboard and the roof of Fred's Fire Truck office is ripped off and blown down the street, leaving a tidal pool on the sales floor. Not good, but you can recover.

Here is where the magic happens. In a matter of hours, your VoIP phones can be redirected to your employee's home or cell phones, and your ERP server, and any other critical server, can be booted up in the cloud. (You did read the previous sections about cloud and virtualization, right?) Now, from the comfort of their own homes, still in their footie pajamas, your sales staff can still be moving product, while the construction company is moving your roof back in place. A month later, you are back in your building, back on your phones, back on your server, and you missed nary a sale. The price of the BDR device looks downright cheap now, doesn't it?

This model is often referred to as business continuity, and you can see why. I would encourage you explore it for your business. It doesn't have to be a hurricane to justify the cost. Even one day of idled staff could easily pay for the investment.

Cloud Services

Another way to fortify your business against disaster is to move critical infrastructure systems, such as email and file share services, to the cloud. Also, as you are looking to upgrade your CRM or ERP systems, or any other line-of-business applications, take a good long look at those that offer a cloud version.

As I said earlier, not everything is good for cloud, but many, many things are. By keeping the majority of your business systems in the cloud, your business is less dependent on location and more dependent on people.

Communications Plan

I am not going to go excruciatingly deep into this topic, as you have probably grown tired of reading all of this by now. However, when my business was impacted by a severe regional tornado outbreak in 2011, I really wish we had spent some time beforehand to have created a communications plan, at a minimum.

During that event, our first priority was our people, and without a good communications plan, we did not know if our employees and their families were safe or in need of some assistance. That was a helpless feeling.

I would advocate putting together a formalized communications plan, even if is simply a redundant call-tree, putting it on paper, and giving every key player a laminated copy to put in their wallet or purse. Make sure your mangers know their staff's phone numbers and addresses, alternate points-of-contact, or anything that might help you verify their well-being.

Also consider setting up Facebook and Twitter accounts so that you can mass-notify your employees of any emergent information.

Once you have verified that everyone is safe, then you can start getting your business put back together.

9 Wrapping it All Up

Throughout this book I have made an effort to explain what I feel is essential for you as a small business owner or manager to understand regarding IT management. Admittedly, there is a lot to it, and certainly a lot more than I have covered here. By now, though, you should be getting a sense of what is involved.

Even if you don't feel that you understand a lot of it, don't fret. What you really need to understand is covered early in the book in the chapter on How to Choose an IT Service Provider. That chapter gives you the right questions to ask and the right things to look for when making the selection. Find a provider who speaks in plain, non-technical language, one that offers those essential services your business needs, and one that shows a commitment to your business success. If you can identify those traits in a provider, then you need not rely on this, or any other IT book.

Acknowledgements

I would like to first thank my wife and editor, Sharon Brown, for making me look less a fool on paper. My public appearance, however, may be something she can't fix.

To Tab Rogers for her continued support, friendship, and loyalty.

To Brad Miller for helping me pursue my business goals, of which this book is a part.

To Kimberly Collette for her friendship, encouragement, and generous offers of help.

I would also like to thank the following individuals/companies for their generous offer of technical advice regarding the content in this book:

James Idle
CelereTech, Inc.
Algonquin, Illinois
http://www.celeretech.com

Tim Meadow
Synergistic, LLC
Victoria, Texas
http://www.synergisdic.com

Jason Marilla
Axiom IT Consulting Canada
North York, Ontario
http://www.axiomcan.com

Lastly, I would like to thank Robin Robins and the staff at Technology Marketing Toolkit, as well as all of the Toolkit members who generously participate in the QUE, having inspired me to take on this project.

About the Author

Scott Brown is a lifelong computer nerd and serial entrepreneur. He has been involved with computers as a primary vocation for over 35 years and still finds them fascinating. Scott has co-owned two technology companies over the last decade and a half, and is now is the sole owner and President of his third business, Ryan Creek Technology Associates, Inc., a Managed IT Service provider north-central Alabama. Visit Ryan Creek Technology online at *ryancreektechnology.com*.

Index

M

malware, 62, 63, 64, 65, 68, 84
Managed Services, 7, 14, 15, 16
mobile device, 49, 50, 51, 52, 59, 70, 72, 75, 80, 81, 84, 85
Mobile Device Management, 50, 72, 73
monitoring, 14, 15, 16, 22, 24, 26, 44, 79, 87, 88

N

network separation, 70

P

passcode, 74, 86
passwords, 9, 22, 70, 74, 76, 78, 80, 86, 96
PBX, 54, 55, 58
Pinterest, 45, 46
Platform as a Service (PaaS), 41
portal, 31, 32
POTS, 54, 55, 56, 57, 58, 59
PRI, 54, 55, 56, 58, 59

R

Recovery Point Objective (RPO), 34, 35, 36, 37
Recovery Time Objective (RTO), 36, 37, 39
refresh plan, 90, 92, 93
refresh planning, 89
remote access, 97
restore, 13, 15, 24, 36, 37, 39, 96

S

security measures, 66, 83, 84
service provider, 19, 20, 21, 22, 24, 25, 88, 96, 103
SIP, 55, 58
social media, 45, 46, 47, 48, 66, 67
Software as a Service (SaaS), 41, 42
SPAM, 47, 65, 66, 79

T

tape, 13, 24, 34, 35, 36, 38, 39, 40, 99
telework, 31, 32, 33, 43
training, 11, 66, 68, 84, 87
Two-Factor Authentication, 74, 75

U

unauthorized software, 87
Unified Threat Management, 62, 64

V

vCIO, 15
virtualization, 27, 28, 29, 30, 31, 37, 40, 42, 96, 100
VoIP, 53, 54, 56, 57, 58, 59, 93, 99
VPN, 31, 32, 33
vulnerabilities, 86

Y

YouTube, 45, 46

www.ingramcontent.com/pod-product-compliance
Lightning Source LLC
Chambersburg PA
CBHW071223050326
40689CB00011B/2429